KILL YOUR TEACHER

Corruption and Racism in Los Angeles City Schools

By
Nachum Shifren

Kill Your Teacher
Corruption and Racism in Los Angeles City Schools

By Nachum Shifren

© 2006 Nachum Shifren

ISBN 0-9786418-0-9

SAN: >>>>>>>>>   8 5 1 – 1 9 0 X   <<<<<<<<<<<<

Library of Congress Control Number: 2006928353

Published by:
Heaven Ink Publishing
P.O. Box 214
Santa Monica, Ca 90406

www.killyourteacher.com

rabbisurf@aol.com

Front/back cover design: Pninah Gilbert-McNabb

Quantity discounts available to groups, organizations or for fundraising

*Part of the profits from **Kill Your Teacher** will go to the Dorsey High Athletic/Scholar Foundation*

What they're saying about Rabbi Shifren's "Kill Your Teacher"

"We now live in a world of Columbine-style school violence, on-campus gang violence, racial and sexual violence, and student-on-teacher violence that has made our schools (especially inner city schools) more like correctional institutions focused on physical misbehavior control than institutions dedicated to learning. "Kill Your Teacher" is not a how-to manual for abusing classroom instructors. It is a warning to us all that inept and corrupt school administration policies are exacerbating the risks to the safety and learning environment of teachers and their students. Rabbi Nachum Shifren writes with the special expertise and first-hand knowledge gained from having been a Los Angeles public school teacher teaching Spanish since 1991. Exposing what he has witnessed with over virulent Black/Hispanic and Black/Anglo racism in the student bodies of these schools, 'Kill Your Teacher' is sobering reading and will prove a substantial contribution to the national dialogue currently underway concerning issues of safety, race relations, and moral clarity within the context of our public school systems and administrative policies."

James A. Cox
Editor-in-Chief
Midwest Book Review

"In chilling and vivid words, Rabbi Shifren has described the depths to which public education has sunk in urban districts like Los Angeles. His recollections as a teacher, engaged in near trench warfare in LA's urban schools should cause the reader to question further public support for a corrupt system that encourages dysfunction and tolerates violence. Shifren's account adds vivid context to the daily multicultural nonsense that erodes common American values and encourages racial and ethnic Balkanization. His book, written in everyday language, is an alarm call that must be heard."

Joe R. Hicks, former executive director of the Southern Christian Leadership Conference

"One of the unfortunate spin-offs from the Civil Rights Movement in the U.S. to repair slave and racist-induced damages done to American Blacks was politically correct speech. When I and other Black students were integrated into White high schools, teachers found it very difficult to manage their classrooms as a result of being afraid to chastise us. When they attempted to do so, Black students would respond with accusations of racism with remarks like, 'You're picking on me because I'm Black!' While these students would escape rebuke designed to increase our learning skills, we suffered in the long term in that we became wild and unruly, causing troubles that our school never had before.

"Low grades and violence resulted in the termination of night athletic competition such as basketball and football, with armed security patrolling the halls of our schools.

"I like Rabbi Shifren because he is willing to continue to break down the wall of political correctness for the sake of saving our children from themselves, and adults in the system who are too selfish and fearful to stand up for what they know is right.

"It is my sentiment that Rabbi Shifren has been given the great task of removing the waves of ignorance destroying our children and to raise the standard of courage that will inspire myriads of other teachers like him to step forward as he has done."

Ted Hayes, Global Homeless and Youth Activist

"Rabbi Shifren's book, 'Kill Your Teacher,' is not just a horrifying expose into the insidious threat of 'multiculturalism' and 'diversity' in our public schools. It is frankly a manifesto of how we can save our youth from the present corrupted educational system. America's educators must make a decision: will we kowtow to forces seeking to balkanize us along racial, class, and ethnic lines, or will we be strengthened through our heritage of belief in G-d and our national values of language and culture?

" Shifren's book is a crossing of the Rubicon, a strategy of delearning previous liberal and un-American agendas of empowerment and social promotion, to finally debate the essence of what it means to be an American."

Shawn Steel

"When those patriots in today's cultural war have prevailed over those who seek to tear from us the values that made this nation great, it will be remembered that Rabbi Shifren led the charge against the evils of 'multiculturalism' and 'diversity.'

"Banished from his teaching position in L.A. schools for daring to raise the academic bar and individual accountability, shunned by his liberal colleagues for his out-spokenness, and attacked by racist administrators of all colors, his was the shot over the bow in bringing sanity back into the classroom. His story, 'Kill Your Teacher,' is one that every concerned American must read!"

George Putnam, Godfather of Talk Radio

"As a former public school teacher in Southern California (Bellflower High School), a pastor, someone who has worked with teenagers for over twenty years, I concur with everything Rabbi Shifren writes about in 'Kill Your Teacher,' which is a must read for every parent, every public school employee, and every politician in our nation.

"Rabbi Shifren, thanks for standing on principle and thanks for writing this much needed book."

Pastor Johnny Esposito
Vice President, Pacific Baptist Bible College

"While I do not discount your experiences or deny the problem you identify, I do not endorse your book as a whole, as I do not agree with your recommendations. Your politics are way too right-wing for me."

Maize Woodford
Editor, The Black Scholar

"I thoroughly endorse Rabbi Shifren's battle on behalf of our nation's students."

William A. Rusher
United Media

"I endorse Rabbi Shifren's book, 'Kill Your Teacher.' His voice on the subject of the degradation of our schools is important and needed."

Senator Fred Hemmings
Hawaii

"Rabbi Shifren and I have shared the joy of surfing the waves off the California coast. As a surfer he rides waves, a waterman who leaves me in awe. As a patriot and dedicated educator, he makes waves. His book, 'Kill Your Teacher', reveals the hidden storm engulfing America's public schools, destroying for the children of middle class and less fortunate families the opportunity for a decent education.

"Would be that Rabbi Shifren's experience in the Los Angeles school system was a fluke, a rare set of circumstances that resulted in a horror story. Instead, his book is a warning that public education in America's cities is a nightmare. It is time to recognize the harm the liberal education establishment is doing and to act before it is too late."

Congressman Dana Rohrabacher

Also by Rabbi Nachum Shifren:

"Surfing Rabbi: A Kabbalistic Quest for Soul"

"Rabbi Nachum Shifren's vehicle is love of the oceans.
Accomplished surfer and devout Jew that he is, he touches
people who would most probably never encounter a rabbi,
let alone an Orthodox one. By exuding a love of life and
joy in the natural world as G-d's creation, the Surfing
Rabbi becomes a living ode to G-d and the Creator. This is
his story. It is a good and inspiring one."

--Dennis Prager

"Fascinating, ultimately important...a spiritual autobiography as compelling and original as its author."

--Michael Medved

"Rabbi Shifren's search for the perfect wave turns into the
ultimate journey, a search for one's soul. His thoughts embrace the sea, the earth and his reflections of the times that
shaped his quest. Just like the sport he cherishes, his life is
about riding the energy of the universe."

--Ira Opper, surf film cinematographer

"Gentiles, Jews, and secular beach rats of all stripe will
find adventure here."

--Scott Hulet, editor, "The Surfer's Journal"

Go to the website: www.surfingrabbi.com

KILL YOUR TEACHER

INTRODUCTION

To write a book like this is difficult. Some have said that it took courage. I am neither a paragon of courage, nor virtue. I believe I am a teacher of ability, who remembers his roots as a youngster in that most unique time of human history, my youth, where our public schools were the envy of the world and academic excellence thrived.

It is necessary for me to thank my wonderful teachers at Reseda High School. Many years ago, it was Mr. Maxwell, who told us, inexplicably, "if you want to understand the homework, you have to turn off the TV!"

It was Mr. Salazar, my dear Spanish teacher, who failed me--not because I did poorly (I got "A's" on all the tests)--but because I didn't dot my "i's" and cross my "t's." Through hard work, I managed a "B" at the end of the semester.

Mr. McConnel instilled within us (completely against our will) a love of the magic of lyric poetry.

Mr. Pinto, of blessed memory, our history teacher, recognized a change in the winds that had started to blow in those turbulent 60's, and with his bow-tie and crew-cut hair, was ever the stickler for standards, never lowering the bar.

To my coaches, Jay and Binder--you taught me the makings of a man. Every marathon or long-distance swim I ever took, I have you to thank for your unceasing wit, sarcasm, roguish sense of humor and absolute love through hard work and sweat.

Looking across this great land, contemplating the absolutely intractable quandaries of educating a youth so removed from the values and building blocks of character that were inculcated in us as we grew up, I realize only now how lucky I am. My teachers were filled with enthusiasm, dedicated, and aware of the difference between right and wrong.

During these dark days, when a nebulous moral curtain draws over our classrooms, and teachers feel pressure to mold curricula and standards to an alien apparition of culture and values, I am strengthened by my mentors who gave of themselves so we could understand the greatness of America.

May G-d continue to bless this great country and all those educators who continually give of themselves so we can know the awesome responsibility of being an American.

January 18, 2006
Rabbi Nachum Shifren

KILL YOUR TEACHER

KILL YOUR TEACHER

FOREWORD by Rabbi Nachum Shifren:

After the first death threat I received from one of my students I should have been shocked. I wasn't. Threats, curses, and humiliating epithets had become routine in the classroom. No amount of referrals to counselors or parent contacts were able to curb the virulent animosity on the part of my student. What DID shock me, however, was seeing his name plastered around campus, shortly thereafter, announcing his candidacy for student body elections ("Change our school, vote for me!" was his campaign slogan). Each time I caught sight of his sheepish grin on the hallway bulletin board, a shudder would go up my spine.

It is the knowledge that, as a public school teacher in an innercity school, I am impotent, actually a captive to absolute corruption with no recourse. This is what is so hard to deal with, the fact that it is of no consequence to anyone that my civil rights are trampled upon, my life put in danger. Ultimately, the administration will remain indifferent and callous to any thought of punishment or redress.

"F... you, you Jewish bastard, I'm going to kill you!" I wonder, what if the roles were reversed. No doubt about it, I'd be tarred and feathered in this town. But there's that face of my student-- a constant reminder of the hidden, hypocritical agenda and the nightmarish dilemma I face each day I go to work. Who cares about the meltdown of civility in our schools? Certainly not the police, whose report has yet to be completed. Certainly not the administration, whose political correctness is palpable. The student was "ordered" to stay away from my building. The day after the incident, I nearly bumped into him in the hall. When I half-heartedly mentioned this to the principal, her overly polite reply indicated that it would be "checked out."

I'm an old-fashioned teacher, brought up during a time when the teacher asked a student to remain seated, the student naturally did so. There was respect, a flag in the classroom, and "one Nation under G-d." I'm not naïve, yet I'm incredulous as to the blatant disruptions, harassing of students by bullies, and crude, abusive language that seems to be the norm. "That's how they are," an African American colleague of mine quipped in reference to the behavior of innercity youth.

Things went South for me the first week of school. I presented a list of class rules and the consequences-- all standard procedure. Suddenly there were questions raised about my assigning detention and paper pick-up after school. Too many students, it seems, were being referred to the dean. If at times the ambiance in the class resembled a war zone, I was nonetheless determined not to let things become TOO hysterical, and made huge efforts, alongside with hours of phone calls home, to maintain a scholarly atmosphere in the class.

I came to class one day to find our building had burned and was severely damaged. Arsonists (students) had started a fire, gutting my class and rendering the entire wing unusable. Then the first warning came. My principal, holding a stack of "complaints about me" in the form of letters, revealed that "word on the street has it that this is payback for your treatment of the students." This bit of news taught me an important lesson: If the kids don't like the failing grade they received, they can burn or destroy at will. Never mind the millions of dollars worth of damage, or the brazen, criminal attack on our campus. I'm looking in my rollbook, scratching my head: Over 50% failures, no homework, no classwork, massive tardiness and absenteeism. What grade was I going to give these students? After all, I had offered my recess time for tutorials, and nobody came.

"Mr. Shifren," the principal continued, with an earnest look on her face. "You've got to be more flexible, more respectful of the children's humanity." Children? These were 12th graders, some of whom would soon be fighting for their country. Why are students allowed to come to my class without notebooks, pencils, paper? Where did they learn that I'm supposed to accept that they come to class whenever they want, and then keep quiet about open defiance toward class rules? But of course, I'm the problem.

"I'm assigning you to the district's classroom management seminar. You obviously have no control over your class," she concluded.

The dean's office is a revolving door. Students sent for brazen defiance, insulting the teacher or preventing others from learning are sent back with a note saying, "student counseled."

"Mr. Shifren, you may not prevent our students from receiving an education. You may not send them out of the class," she continued her accounting of "don'ts." This was, more than anything else that she could have done, my death sentence. It was her way of telling me to take my standards for class decorum and shove it. If there's a problem, then it is me. And if I can't handle it, I can quit.

Humanity? I was shocked when one day, a hysterical woman, a community liaison, barged into class with a student that I had sent to the office not a minute earlier. He was referred for wandering around the class, harassing other students. "I'm sick of you kicking out all the black students!" But all I HAVE are black students. No apology was made by the principal. I sent a letter requesting that harassment against me cease, or release me if I'm found to be a bigot.

There is something sinister about my experiences here. We're being asked to remove all fences around basic human conduct. What's wrong, is right. Despicable levels of discourse, defiance and disrespect have become the order of the day. And it's not just in my school. Who will tell them the truth, that they're being promoted without any skills, any sense of civic or individual responsibility. This is the REAL racism that our educational establishment hasn't the nerve to face up to.

I met a colleague who had learned of the death threat against me. In a moment of unusual levity, he offered, "Don't lose any sleep over it. As long as you're still alive, be sure to get your semester grades in on time."

Of course I will.

KILL YOUR TEACHER

KILL YOUR TEACHER

Table of Contents

To the Editor of the Los Angeles Times:

I have been a language teacher with the Los Angeles
Unified School District since 1991. Today I will sign a
final agreement after an exhaustive grievance process, in
which I will never be allowed to teach in the District again.
For its part, the District will remove my negative teacher
performance evaluation.

During my last two years at Dorsey High, I've had my
classroom burnt to the ground, had a death threat, physical
assaults, and constant accusations of racism. Community
"activists" in our area have written woeful letters to the
Superintendent, imploring her to remove me from my
position as a Spanish teacher. Their accusation: Students
are failing my class because they're forced to learn Greek
and Hebrew instead of Spanish.

I've endured countless demeaning "parent conferences"
where lack of student comportment and academic
achievement was inevitably spun into my "lack of
classroom management and INSENSITIVITY TO THE
NEEDS OF A DIVERSE STUDENT POPULATION."

Students who did little or no homework, refusing to turn
in term papers and not having passed a single exam, were
able to manipulate conferences with allegations of racism
or personal animosity.

When students were sent from my room to the Dean's
office for outrageous behavior, such as stabbing another
student with a pencil, obnoxious epithets or racial slurs,
and open defiance directed against the teacher, they would
never arrive; instead, they were picked up by security
(found walking around the campus) while our ever-
resourceful administration documented a "clear lack of
student-teacher rapport and managerial skills."

The picture I've painted becomes clearer when one
considers that the student who threatened to kill me was
allowed to run for student body office! If I had any doubts
about my stature on our campus, they were dispelled by
such overt attitudes such as this.

Despite numerous excellent references and observations
on the part of counselors, mentor teachers, and coaches
about my dedication to upholding high academic standards
and maintaining a high level of student responsibility
and values, I spent two years in a hostile environment
without respite from community or administration.
Only two individuals came to my assistance during
this nightmare: Rev. Jesse Lee Peterson, community
activist and director of BOND International, and
Congressman Dana Rohrabacher of Huntington Beach.
Congressman Rohrabacher was sufficiently convinced of
egregious nature of campus relations that he contacted
Superintendent Roy Romer for clarification. He was
stonewalled again and again, with each inquiry going
unanswered (the Superintendent was either on vacation
or too busy to get back to the Congressman-- this over
a period of several months and many messages left by
staff). Rev. Peterson was present at one of my grievance
hearings and was moved to make the comment that I could
never get a fair hearing from my administrator since in his
words, "She is a blatant racist."

Yet there is a deep sadness in me, a feeling of
disconnectedness from the many students with whom I
was fortunate enough to befriend, impacting their lives
with a sense of a world built on achievement, maximum
effort, and tireless academic rigor.

As I told the District Superintendent during my last stage
of the grievance process, I forgive the death threats,
the physical assaults, the demeaning and racial slurs

hurled at me by my charges. If they didn't have the
support of "activists" and malevolent do-gooders intent
on re-addressing perceived wrongs and power trips by
"outsiders" toward their community, this despicable
behavior and attitude never would have occurred. In
several cases, stacks of letters of complaints were waved at
me by my principal (I was never allowed to see the letters
or respond to them) as proof that I was not getting along
with my students. She offered this as the justification for
burning down my classroom.

It will be hard for me to reconcile with an administration
bent on political correctness that serves to ramrod a
concerned and caring teacher right out of the District.

My union rep told me frankly that I was "the wrong man in
the wrong community." This is what hurts me most of all.
I gave it my best, taking students with severe emotional
and family problems, tempering them with a sense of
achievement for a job well done: "You missed the deadline
for the term paper? It's OK, your grade won't be as high as
it should, but just get it in to me as soon as you can-- with
spelling and grammar checked...."

Around campus, the many students who didn't manage
to pass my class would greet me each morning, ask how
things are going-- each of them knowing that ultimately, I
was on their side. I will miss my students, and I know that
they won't forget me.

DANA ROHRABACHER
46th District, California

Committees:
INTERNATIONAL RELATIONS
Chairman, Subcommittee on
Oversight and Investigations
Subcommittee on
Asia and the Pacific

SCIENCE
Subcommittee on
Space and Aeronautics
Subcommittee on Research

Congress of the United States
House of Representatives

April 27, 2004

WASHINGTON OFFICE:
2338 Rayburn House Office Building
Washington, DC 20515-0546
(202) 225-2415 FAX: (202) 225-0145

DISTRICT OFFICE:
101 Main Street, Suite 380
Huntington Beach, CA 92648-8118
(714) 960-6483 FAX: (714) 960-7806

South Bay: (310) 377-9493

http://rohrabacher.house.gov

The Hon. Roy Romer
Superintendent
Los Angeles Unified School District
333 South Beaudry Avenue
Los Angeles, California 90017-1466

Dear Superintendent Romer:

I am writing this letter on behalf of Nachum Shifren, who teaches Spanish at Dorsey High School in the Los Angeles Unified School District. I was shocked to learn that Mr. Shifren will not be rehired for the school year 2004-2005, despite the fact that Mr. Shifren has been teaching in the district since 1991 and has a superlative teaching record.

I have known Mr. Shifren for several years and can vouch for his concern for his students and their academic proficiency. His teaching style relies upon standards and accountability, a technique that is all too rare in many of our schools anymore. I have received many letters testifying to the quality of his teaching ability. Knowing Mr. Shifren as I do, I am not surprised that he is held in such high esteem.

I am worried that undue pressure has been put on Mr. Shifren's school and district administrators by community "activists," who seem to be displeased that Mr. Shifren demands hard work and accountability for his students. I am told that among other absurd charges, Mr. Shifren stands accused of teaching "Greek and Hebrew" to his students. Mr. Shifren has shown me a log of phone conversations with many of the parents of his students, attesting to their gratitude for his intervention in the lives of their children. I think that, among other things, rebuts any claim that Mr. Shifren is anything less than a superb teacher.

His record is all the more remarkable for the fact that during his tenure at Dorsey he has endured death threats and acts of arson against his classroom. Unlike others who would have reacted differently, he has not abandoned this difficult outpost. It is clear that in addition to his aptitude for teaching, he has a passion for it as well.

I am following Mr. Shifren's situation closely and am greatly disturbed by this development. I'd be very grateful if you would call me at my office at (202) 225-2415 and share with me your insights about this matter.

Sincerely,

Dana Rohrabacher
Member of Congress

After 33-years service in capacity of classroom teacher
and administrator for the second largest school district in
America (Los Angeles Unified), it is with authority I vali-
date Rabbi Shifren's assessments in Kill Your Teacher.

Any teacher worth his salt having worked in "inner-city"
(black and Hispanic) schools, can attest to much the same
student activities and administration actions/inactions/reac-
tions of which Rabbi Shifren reports. Few would have the
courage of Rabbi Shifren to publicly do so.

Recently, Lou Dobbs of CNN, presented Americans with
some disturbing facts on our schools. Among which, 50%
of black and Hispanic teenagers do not graduate from high
school. As Rabbi Shifren points out, teachers are encour-
aged to pass minority (i.e. black and Hispanic) students
who did not work for excellence. Students quickly learn
they do not have to study for learning or passing grades,
finishing high school with spurious diplomas.

Let us not think dumbing down of our students is limited
to blacks and Hispanics. Articles galore have been written
on why "Johnny can't read." According to latest accounts,
"Johnny can't read, write or think." Even though research
has been done on "why Johnny's teachers can't teach,"
none has been as inclusive as Rabbi Shifren's Kill Your
Teacher.

It is not uncommon in countries which celebrate group
rights over individual freedoms to live and believe in the
concept "it takes a village to raise a child." But in America, vast numbers agree with syndicated columnist Mark
Thornhill: It takes parents whose authority isn't undermined by meddling government socialists to raise a child.

In this country, we celebrated individual rights; until
the advent of "diversity" and "multiculturalism" in our

schools. Diversity and multi-culturalism do nothing more than promote hatred for America and bigotry among ethnic groups. Examples of this divisiveness abound with reports of black and white students fighting over refusals of blacks to honor the American Flag, whites flying the Confederate Flag; black and Hispanic students fighting because one has "dissed" (disrespected) the other's culture.

America's public schools should be in the business of teaching American culture. The teaching of American history (true not revised), the United States Constitution, and civic responsibility is a must for all our children--no matter their color, financial status, ethnicity.

Rabbi Shifren sought to provide his students with a classroom atmosphere conducive to learning. Refusing to support him in this regard, school authority evidently thought students did not deserve such a learning environment. Rabbi Shifren wanted to give his students meaningful lessons: not just read but read with comprehension; not just write but write with greater clarity, style and substance; not just compute but utilize critical thinking and analytic reasoning. From their treatment of Rabbi Shifren and teachers of his ilk, school authority and teacher unions and "community activists" are content with "feel-good" lessons.

Do parents really know what their children are suffering through on a daily basis in the government schools?

First, the Federal government has no business (according to the Constitution) funding and dictating curricula for public schools. The highest quality education in America was before the Federal government took control of the schools. Quality has steadily declined ever since.

Secondly, "community activists" have no place in our schools. They do not represent the best interest of parents and their children. Most, if not all, these community activists are paid accomplices of local "politically ambitious" school board members and politicians using our children to promote their socialist agenda.

For every freedom-loving American, Kill Your Teacher is a must-read. Every American citizen, with or without school-age children, must recognize our future is determined by today's education. It really is true, an educated people is a free people.

For those Americans unaware of the direction today's education is taking us -- incapacity rather than talent, despotism instead of liberty, vice over virtue, ignorance above enlightenment

I strongly suggest you read Kill Your Teacher.

EZOLA FOSTER

Black Americans for Family Values
Founder/Past President
2000 Election Vice President Candidate
First Black Woman to run on major party ticket

As someone who is in regular contact with students and teachers in the Los Angeles area, I can tell you that the Los Angeles Unified School District-- and the rest of our government school system-- is in shambles. It is filled with politically correct, godless socialists, who are daily remaking our children in their own image.

Amongst this wreckage, a good friend of mine, Rabbi Nachum Shifren, decided to make a difference, and install discipline, standards, and excellence where there were none. His reward for that was a heap of abuse.

Rabbi Shifren invited me to speak one day to his class, in the hopes that I, as a black American, could possibly reach some of the minority students who so despised Rabbi Shifren, a white, Jewish man, and let them know how to succeed in life.

What I found was that I was not respected either. Because I represented authority, and this generation has been taught by their Leftist mentors to "question authority," meaning treat it with suspicion and even contempt.

In Rabbi Shifren's classroom, I found out that only a handful actually had two parents in the home, meaning the battle was mostly lost before these kids hit a classroom. Most of the students displayed no interest in learning whatsoever, and were hostile. The classroom was an unsafe environment to good teachers like Rabbi Shifren.

Soon after my visit there, I learned that Rabbi Shifren's classroom had been burnt down under highly suspicious circumstances. No surprise.

What a disappointment to see a good teacher really attempt to educate, yet receive no support from the Administration and teacher's union (U.T.L.A.). Instead of support, they fought him at every turn!

The American people must wake up to what is being done in the government schools with their money! They are supporting re-education camps for children and teenagers. They must stop supporting this wanton destruction of our sons and daughters, and start supporting teachers like Rabbi Shifren who are standing up for discipline, standards, and excellence in an atmosphere of chaos.

Many of our young people do want to learn, and excel. They need to be given that chance. The administrators, teachers, and students who are "bad apples" need to be removed, for the sake of the good ones.

I know that if we had ten more teachers like Rabbi Nachum Shifren, we could turn America around tomorrow.

--Rev. Jesse Lee Peterson
  Founder and President, BOND

February 7, 2006

Rabbi Nachum Shifren's new book "Kill Your Teacher" is an expose of the first order relative to the "dumbing down" of our Public School Students.

From this study, one easily sees a need for Americans to wake up. The night is far spent; the day is at hand. Rabbi Shifren masterfully brings out the fact that community "activists" demanding diversity really, in essence, mean reverse-racism.

What is needed, as is pointed out by the studious Rabbi, is an old-fashioned house cleaning, really getting to the problems at hand, rather than the obfuscation and posturing producing a superficial situation based on appearances. The problem of education has festered and festered for many years, and those supposed groups and individuals in our educational process – the NEA and other supposed educational groups – continue to fatten themselves to the detriment of American Public School Kids.

Constantly, we see (as does the good Rabbi) youngsters reaching the boiling point in their frustrations when not having academic averages commensurate to graduation, causing the necessity of going to summer schools and losing hoped-for athletic scholarships due to bad grades.

This is a must read for parents and educators!!!!!!

Jim Vineyard
Pastor – Windsor Hills Baptist Church
Oklahoma City, Oklahoma

JAV:sgb

"Teacher," the very word conjures up memories of people who were always there to help me. I had been one of those children who needed a little extra help to learn to read. Bless all teachers that taught me that, and more. Reading Rabbi Shifren's account on what he had to go through at the hands of those who should have been there to help him, is beyond words.

What was done to Rabbi Shifren and other teachers who dare speak the truth will be remembered with shame in this nation. We need to come to grips with the fact that there are those that want to destroy America from within.

Rabbi Shifren's book "Kill Your Teacher" must be read to understand what has happened to our once great California School System.

California's schools have gone from being the best in the nation, to being the worst in the nation. Children are leaving our schools without knowing how to read or write simple sentences. Illiteracy has become the norm. Those that make it through the system often find themselves going to remedial classes in college. Or worse, they find they're incapable of functioning in society, not being able to get a job or fill out a simple application.

I am humbled and honored to have met Rabbi Shifren and applaud his efforts to bring the truth to light in his book.

Blessings,
Lupe Moreno
President,
Latino Americans for Immigration Reform
City of Santa Ana, Library Commissioner

KILL YOUR TEACHER

Corruption and Racism in Los Angeles City Schools

By
Nachum Shifren

"F...you, Jewish bastard, I'm going to kill you!" The threats, assaults, humiliations and institutional racism of Dorsey High seem like some long-ago nightmare. One year's passage however, has not healed wounds that run deep. The hurt of being abandoned by those who I thought were there for support (my paid Union rep!), thrown to the mercy of an administration bent on obfuscation of any racial tensions is still so incredible to me. I contacted Larry Elder, Michael Savage, Rush Limbaugh, in short, any right-wing talk show host that could help me get some payback. Not even one call was returned.

Nobody believed me! When I filed the police report about the death threat, my principal's reaction was shocking: "Frankly, Mr. Shifren, it's your word against his! You know, this kind of thing happens all the time in politics!"

Congressman Dana Rohrabacher stepped up to the plate on my behalf calling the Superintendent of Schools, Roy Romer. He faxed him, e-mailed, and left countless messages through his Washington staff, attempting to arrange a meeting to deal with the lawlessness at Dorsey. For weeks, Romer was either in the Caribbean on vacation or simply unavailable.

"I am an L.A.U.S.D. teacher who's received a death threat!" I screamed at the secretary, who I knew was an accessory to the stonewalling superintendent.

The teacher's union? After working in the District for nearly 20 years, I could have predicted the cozy relationship between them both. There will never be any waves made by these left-wing advocates of the current political correctness debasing our students. For sure not in a case where a white teacher is being harassed by an African-American principal. There's an unwritten law: If you're white, there are no issues about race: How would it look for the union to be pushing an issue of anti-white racism?

I was in a situation not unlike Selma, Alabama in the 60's: I am a Black man, hung out to dry by the system with nowhere to go. If the situation was reversed, and a Black man was being discriminated against, Kofi Annan would have been helicoptered to Dorsey to "assess" the situation.

It all started in my first month in the Fall of 2003. I made it clear that as a Spanish teacher, I would be assigning homework daily and that the success of the course would be tied to the performance, and the timely turning in of these assignments. After all, there can be no proceeding ahead with language skills without mastery of previous lessons studied.

Less than fifty percent of the class complied. This in itself is a grave issue. More disturbing was class demeanor of a select group of students bent on torpedoing any modicum of learning atmosphere. No paper, pencil, or books were brought to class. Instead, many students spent inordinate amounts of time "borrowing"-- chronically-- necessary items from others, thereby halting the pace of the lessons dead in its tracks.

Despite rules clearly posted, many students seemed to think that there were no consequences for disruptive and rude behavior. They were right! When after several warnings, notes and phone calls home to parents they were sent to the dean for disciplinary action, they returned to class, literally in a revolving-door fashion. Their signed referrals were nearly always the same: "Student counseled. This is not a matter for the Dean's office. Refer to your teacher manual." Indeed, there were no drugs sold, nor was anyone assaulted! No grounds here for any involvement on the part of the administration. Here is the teacher's nightmare: You can either reconcile yourself to the sneers, the rudeness, that "attitude" ("don't tell me

what to do, White man!")-- knowing full well there is no
leverage available to modify these types of behavior-- or
you can quit. Many teachers choose the latter. The rate of
attrition at Dorsey that year was thirty to forty percent.
The administration is banking on your getting completely
burned out and exhausted. It is so much easier for them to
send the teacher packing than to do the difficult legwork of
providing a no-nonsense academic environment.

　　　Here is the true racism in the presumption that
inner city kids cannot be expected to complete homework
(nor come in for tutoring which was provided in my class
on a daily basis), sit down in assigned seats (without
wandering around the room, disrupting others trying to
learn), and display proper conduct toward the teacher and
others.

　　　In grading papers and tests, I would have to lower
grades for many improper uses of grammar-- the most
common, double negatives. It cannot be overstated that the
absolute breakdown in proper use of the English language
was endemic-- and completely tolerated. Here was another
point of contention, pitting myself squarely against
students, administration, and community "activists," more
than happy to settle for the abysmally low level of the
status quo.

　　　"But Mr. Shifren, their reality is reflected in
their speech and vocabulary. You shouldn't bring them
down on this account," was the shocking admission of a
counselor to me regarding the use of "ain't" and "I been"
in a composition. Frustrated, I remarked that I speak five
languages, and a foreign language is used in my home,
yet I must properly communicate with others in English
in order to effectively live in a multicultural society. My
rationale did not prevail.

　　　I was shocked at the level of filth and audacity
in every-day exchanges between teacher and student.

As always, I presented myself dressed in a suit and tie, establishing from the onset a level of standards based on professionalism. Not only did this demeanor on my part fail to make any impression, it had the effect of "instigating," serving to accentuate differences in attitudes and mindset. I unwittingly was set up as an authoritarian figure, an "outsider" infiltrating the community with an alien belief system, using coercion to have students comply with class rules. Add to this perception my orthodox "Jewish" beard and head covering, and it became a lightning rod in which resentment could be more passionately vented.

At some point, community "activists" started doing their malevolent thing, dredging up archaic visions of classic Jewish/Black antagonisms and issues of divisiveness. In response to breakdowns of class discipline, non-cooperation, uncouth behavior or language, the issue of race and division continually surfaced.

"Why you always wanna keep the Black man down, Shifren?" was an oft-repeated refrain usually heard after a low score on a test or report card.

I'm not trying to keep anyone down. If you'd do your homework, your grade would be higher.

Seat changes were a way to put out small fires of disruption. "Why you always movin' the Black man, but never movin' the Mexicans?" How does a teacher respond to this? More disturbingly, where did the student get it into his head that consequences for misbehavior represented racism?

A slow stream of students ended up in the office for chronic disregard for class rules, failure to bring "notification-to-parents" slips signed, and rude, obnoxious behavior. The principal knows them well; these are the kids that are shuffled around like cards, cast-outs that nobody has the strength or will to deal with. I'm the fall

guy-the teacher who has the temerity to set standards
where there never have been any. In a total vacuum, my
presence was felt at Dorsey and it was not a pleasant one.

After this scenario played itself out for nearly a
month, my classroom was burned down. The resulting
damage went into the hundreds of thousands of dollars,
with adjacent buildings heavily damaged. This impacted
our already stressed-out, overcrowding. For six weeks,
Dorsey teachers were forced to schlep their books, chalk,
erasers and personal items from room to room, their lives
completely disrupted. Our "C" building was roped off
as a hazardous area, with the pungent smell of burned
asbestos lingering as a constant reminder of the episode.
The reaction on the part of the administration? Business
as usual, a mode of denial and obfuscation was the order
of the day, with no attempt on Dr. Mahmud's part to use
this event to catalyze student respect for property and an
increased level of student responsibility. Kids aren't stupid.
Everyone knew that this "burn-baby-burn" mindset was
condoned by Dr. Mahmud as was evidenced by her silence.
Shockingly, students whom I never met would pass me
in the hallways, yelling out, "Hey, Shifren, we heard they
tried to burn you out, guess you'll be looking for another
job!" Tragically, the indifference toward this incitement
and violence resulted in having my respect and stature as
a teacher totally smothered, essentially putting me forever
on the defensive with students and parents. Permeated
in everyone's mind was the feeling that a teacher whose
students so hate him that they feel "compelled" to burn
his classroom down, cannot be taken seriously and is a
liability to both staff and students.

Dr. Mahmud invited me into her office shortly
after my classroom was destroyed. Her mood was somber,
angry, aggressive. I was naïve to think that she would
commiserate with me about this horrific act. Instead, she
raised a stack of papers from her desk, while glaring in my

direction, saying, "Mr. Shifren, I have dozens of letters of complaints about you from concerned parents about your attitude. The common theme seems to be that the students don't like you and feel that they're not learning. Don't you think you should choose some other profession? You're incapable of being a friend of the students, and word on the street has it that your classroom was burned down as a result. If you continue on here at Dorsey, you'll need to be less of a disciplinarian and start reaching out to our students, respecting their cultural diversity and unique backgrounds."

To my pleading that I'm only trying to set and uphold minimum classroom standards and decorum, she was adamant. "You have to back off, stop being so harsh. Let the kids like you, then you can worry about standards. I'm putting you on notice that I'll be making many visits to your area, checking your ability to manage your class and provide a standards-based curriculum. I'll remind you that you are a probationary teacher and will need a positive evaluation from me for tenure in the District."

I knew I was a goner. But why was I not hearing from her some even feigned apology or words of consolation over the outrage that had just occurred. Why was there no fuss about the hundreds of thousands of dollars' damage caused to taxpayers? Where was the deep regret that the situation at Dorsey was so out of control that a mindset had evolved where "burning out" a teacher was justified?

The entire focus was to play down what was actually happening by shifting attention to "class management skills" of the teacher; concentrate on the perceptions of the community "activists" that "racist" or "culturally insensitive" views of the teacher served to alienate students and discourage true learning. Furthermore, Dr. Mahmud's attitude and actions fostered a situation in which my physical safety at Dorsey was jeopardized. At no time did she publicly admonish this sort of reprehensible behavior. Again, if the tables were turned and a Black teacher was "burned out," there would have been a nation-wide soul-searching. Truly, there was a very minimal transition between burning a teacher's classroom and actual physical violence directed at the teacher. At no time did Dr. Mahmud respond to the dozens of referrals sent to her office for rowdiness, verbal threats, and open defiance of class protocols. Screaming, hysterical shouting matches in the hallways, involvement of L.A.P.D. campus security in restraining or removing classroom hooligans were met with total indifference. There was a set-up at work here, in which she tacitly engineered the breakdown of my classroom control and credibility as an educator.

Some of the "activists" were given a position of authority at Dorsey, charged with heading the "Parent Center." They were given an office and staff. Their role was ostensibly to serve as liaison between the parents and the school. What actually entailed was a form of monitoring teachers with whom students were having difficulties. In my two years of teaching at Dorsey I never heard from these activists about an agreed plan of improved student comportment, promises by students to turn in homework, show up on the time with regular attendance, proposals to tutor or otherwise boost student academic performance.

Instead, there evolved a constant state of tension where a revolving door style treatment of egregious cases of classroom breakdown became the standard. Incredibly, just minutes after my referral of a problem student for attempting to stab a classmate with a pencil, this same student re-entered my class along with the parent center rep, screaming (having no compunction about interrupting my lesson-- instead willfully sowing divisiveness and racial animosity), "I'm tired of you kicking out Black kids from your class!" (Who was she to tell me what to do in

the first place? From where did this parent feel the self-
confidence and assuredness to enter a teacher's classroom
and remonstrate him in the midst of a lesson? This not
even the Superintendent is allowed to do). Of course, it
didn't occur to her that all my students were Black.

Here the tactic was laid bare: To put me on notice that,
1) I'm a racist; 2) My referrals could be handled not by
the campus security or the administration, but by partisan
interests with a stake in diluting the effectiveness of
classroom management due to perceived racist sentiments
of the teacher (me). This is a scandal that in any other
institution would result in a formal inquiry into policy
and discrimination. But most outrageous and hurtful of
all is the fact that causing such hysteria in the middle of
my classroom, in the presence of my students, created
a precedent whereby I could be further undermined by
degrading my classroom standards and expectations. After
all, how seriously would my demands be taken that kids
follow the rules when there were no consequences for
breaking them.

Ironically, a continuous claim from the "Parent
Center" was that by my frequent referrals, I was "denying
students educational opportunities." Thus, we could
conclude with similar logic that incarceration of killers
denies them equal access to society's benefits.

This Pandora's box subsequently led to a flood
of letters, instigated by the "Parent Center," to the
Superintendent of Schools, prevailing upon him to remove
me from my teaching position. I was having a "detrimental
effect upon students and community." When I think about
the specious manner in which the letter was composed (I
received a copy only during my grievance hearing, without
having proper time to respond to the absurd allegations), it
would be considered laughable in any normal environment.
Yet, it was used as an essential weapon in my removal
from the district. It was understood that the administration

could not endure constant phone calls and letters from irate parents. There needed to be a lessening of pressure, hence my removal.

But what was so remarkable about one particular letter from the "Parents' Center" was the accusation therein that children were complaining about "not learning anything" (read: poor grades) due to my teaching Hebrew! What was going on here? When was the last time a language teacher was accused of teaching the wrong language? Even if this were true, would not such a charge be checked out first by the administration? And if it was confirmed, there would be no doubt that a warning would be given, putting the teacher on notice. How did such a bizarre accusation become part of the protocol (which was presented as material evidence during my hearing with the Superintendent)?

Here, the "big lie" method was thoroughly applied. To solidify such wild claims one needed only observe my orthodox Jewish demeanor consisting of a long beard and skullcap, with my custom of reading Psalms (in Hebrew) during our Sustained Silent Reading period each morning. The subtle and not so subtle hinting of resentment toward outsiders, or as one Black activist put it, "white interlopers," resonated with each of these raving canards.

When I checked the parents' last names on the complaint letters, matching them with the students, in each case the usual evidence of lack of class participation, goofing off, absence of homework was apparent.

But what of this racist double standard? Are there no Latino English teachers who choose to read papal encyclicals in Spanish or Latin? Are there no Black French teachers who enjoy reading the works of Marcus Garvey or Frederick Douglas? The lengths that the community "activists" went to tar and feather me with their own insidious racist brand of lies was so obtuse and transparent at the same time, that I simply laughed it off, certainly no one reasonable could believe these claims! Not even a corrupt principal such as Dr. Mahmud could have the machinations to link low grades with my teaching the students "Hebrew!" How wrong I was. At my dismissal hearing, the letter was thrown in my face-- for the very first time-- and presented as one of the reasons for my being removed from the District. My UTLA representative was present at the hearing, and could only sheepishly offer, "Rabbi, your misfortune is you're in the wrong school at the wrong time."

My union rep throughout this incident was counter-productive. There's a reason for this. The point of commonality that both the Union and the District share is distancing themselves from public scrutiny and focus of attention in all regards. While this corollary doesn't hold true for Gay, Latino, or Black claims of unfairness (here it is safe to say that in the climate of political correctness, any and all sentiments of unfair treatment to any of these groups is accentuated), it does hold true where Whites are demeaned or discriminated against. Comes along an orthodox Jew and there is absolutely no peer group to offer support.

There's another reason why no attention was ever drawn to the egregious acts of discrimination in my case. We are in a period of "pay-back"-- restitution and over- compensation toward minorities for previous years of injustice. Now is their time-- and their time ONLY. No other claims of activism on behalf of any other minorities are acceptable. When we hear talk of "minorities," it never enters our mind to include in the discussion Armenians, Koreans, Chinese, Filipinos and certainly not Jews.

Really, there is a reverse racism at work. For whatever burr that may be languishing up someone's saddle, a White, conservative Jewish rabbi is the perfect hitching post.

The unspoken code in both Union and District is that Blacks and Hispanics are ALWAYS victims, never aggressors. No, we won't ever discuss gangs and their paralyzing effect on communities and schools. Drugs, sexual promiscuity, dysfunction in academic performances at all levels-- here there are no consequences, no conclusions ever drawn. There's just a white racist, somewhere, somehow, lurking around the corner, manipulating academic failure and social irresponsibility.

The Union and the District, for all the contention they radiate outwardly, conveniently play ball on these issues and are in bed together. The teacher is simply a pawn in the larger game of keeping the parent pacified with a "feel good" attitude relating to all manner of breakdown in the District. Promotion and advancement take precedence to solving urgent problems in the classroom. The last thing administrators want are questioning phone calls from parents, letter writing from activists, or to focus attention on themselves. In no way will solving a teacher's problem come at the expense of tarnishing someone else's image or giving the perception that things are out of control.

Dorsey was beset with riots when the issue of Exit Exams became hot. These are standardized state levels of minimum performance in order to graduate from high school. There are no standards presently--witness the high number of high school graduates (nearly 50%) that are forced to take remedial English in college to make up for skills not mastered in high school. For several hours, hundreds of students were marauding through the campus, causing a school-wide lockdown. LAPD was out in force, helicopters flew overhead. No one was allowed out of their rooms for hours, not even to go to the bathroom. Several of my students were forced to urinate in the hallway. There was real fear for teachers' lives, such was the hysteria. Why? The students know they're not educated and failing.

They know, as do their parents, that if they were to be forced to prove their competence in academic skills, they would fall short of the measure.

Time and time again, I became incredulous about feedback I'd gotten from my students indicating a total lack of basic language skills. Our Spanish class was not the venue for compository writing or involved grammar, yet a basic knowledge of the difference between, for example, subject, adverb, and adjective was essential. Many of my students were unable to satisfactorily demonstrate subject-verb agreement in gender and person-- even by the end of the semester. It's not that the Spanish itself was difficult, rather they failed my class even before it started due to an abysmal failure of our school to insist on upholding standards.

The riots that broke out that day were a response to mounting frustration and alienation of the students. Piddling away their precious hours with inane activities, "busy work," is the road Dorsey had chosen to avoid the critical issues. I saw the uncontrollable rage daily in the faces of my charges. Thrust into a highly technical, extremely competitive society, they are dumbed down by a racist system. Instead of instituting a no-holds-barred educational Marshall Plan to resuscitate the moribund halls of academia, they are fed their yearly pablum of weeks of "ethnic pride" identification a la Martin Luther King and Caesar Chavez. Speakers are invited to Dorsey, admonishing our "racist" society, often taking the kids out of precious class time. Posters flood the campus, calling attention to the very things that divide us.

One of my students, a girl, unexpectedly informed me that she'd be leaving Dorsey. When I probed around her hesitancy in giving a reason, she confided that she was under tremendous peer pressure NOT to get good grades. "People were telling me I was acting too white!" she remarked sadly. Here was a gifted, hard-working student that was forced to move back East, far away from friends and neighborhood, to a place free from victimization and dysfunction.

Too White? This really gives a teacher tremendous enthusiasm and confidence as he or she faces the challenge of raising the bar! The riots at Dorsey symbolized something even more ominous: A violent reaction toward changing business-as-usual. Attempts to alter old behavior patterns and study skills would be met with the same fate. The inference was clear to the teacher, as he heard helicopters and bullhorns screeching overhead. Its real message was: Keep your mouth shut and you won't get hurt.

In my two years at Dorsey, not once was staff development focused on these vital concerns. Smoke and mirrors were the order of the day. One Black activist, an "expert" hired by the District to educate us insensitive White teachers, bemoaned the students being taken to task for poor language skills, calling English the "language of the oppressor." At that same staff development, Catherine Webb, our assistant principal, called for more "movement" in the classroom. "Kids will learn better," she said, if they can dance and utilize ethnic rhythms which would allow them to feel more "participatory." In other words, tradition and learning for the sake of learning, hard work on mastery of skills, were somehow to be identified with the "oppressor," a White cabal designed to stifle minority ethnic self expression.

Here again, a subtle hint to the teacher to back off from rigorous academic expectations. The set-up by the administration here was clear: Don't upset the rotten applecart of lack of skills and unwillingness to be part of mainstream America. This is what Dr. Mahmud meant when she told me that fateful day, after my classroom had been burned down, "Back off, you need to learn to get along with the students." Over and over, I envision her waving that stack of letters by outraged parents demanding my removal from school. Her demeanor, her harsh stare at me, were the shot over the bow in a personal war. I could either meet her tyrannical terms or continue to insist on upholding minimum classroom conduct and academic achievement. But I HAD changed. The "war" needed to move to a different front. Documentation became the order of the day.

One day Dr. Mahmud invited me to her office and scolded me for not contacting a parent. "I got a call stating that the parent had no idea that her daughter has been absent for two months. This is a serious matter." (The whole time I'm thinking: THIS is a serious matter!? But death threats against teachers, assaulting them, burning down their classrooms-- no problem, right?) It was serious because it helped complete the portfolio of the District's contention that I was not up to par as a teacher. Negative feedback by parents automatically translate into harassment and pressure on the teacher. Never mind that notes were sent home and not signed. Never mind that calls home are not answered or picked up by foster parents, grandparents, aunts and uncles. And the like.

"What I'm getting is a pattern of neglect in your duties to keep records and maintain communication with parents. Absences prevent students from achieving their academic goals." The whole "shock" about the student's poor attendance had a hollow ring. The shock was limited only to my class; indeed, low grades and attendance of other classes proved less shocking.

In an effort to open another front on my assault at Dorsey, I took upon myself to create a phone log, noting dates and times of calls home. In addition to my duties at school, and grading homework after school, I was up for nearly two hours every night speaking with parents about deficient conduct and academic performance in my class. Many parents were grateful, saying that they had no idea

WHAT their child was doing in school.

"I ask him how his Spanish class is going and he tells me, 'OK.' I ask him, 'where's your Spanish homework, he tells me they don't get Spanish homework." This was a typical response. Now an additional burden was added to my tactic of covering my rear end from further admonitions from Dr. Mahmud: Daily progress reports detailing class work, quizzes, tests, and homework. These were to be signed by parents. Very few ever were.

"Mr. Shifren, I have a parent on the phone that says you promised to inform her about her child's performance in class, yet she's received no written reports from you. This represents a lack of follow-up on your part." Well, I DID get signatures of the parents, only problem was they were forged.

"Mr. Shifren, I have a parent complaining about your continuous calls home about her child's homework. The parent feels harassed. You need to be sensitive to the feelings of parents-- don't be overbearing." Even my attempts to get the parents involved, shifting the pressure I was under, had backfired. The PARENT felt harassed? What about the chronic harassment of the teacher, enduring daily verbal, degrading assaults of impudence?

Another "shocked" parent instituted a series of parent-teacher conferences after several failures on report cards. I had a mile-long list of phone calls made home: grandma, aunts, uncles-- but where was the parent? Did the parent give a damn about her kid, or was this her way of venting on the teacher, a stress-release for her pent-up frustrations as a result of a complete breakdown in her responsibilities as a parent. One of the hot issues that surfaced during our more than five conferences (these would extend from the beginning of my one hour pupil-free conference period through the nutrition break which was 20 minutes long. It was a cruel joke! Nonetheless, Dr.

Mahmud, always taking copious notes, with a grim look
on her face, added an immeasurable amount of melodrama
for the sake of the parent) with this parent, abetted by
Dr. Mahmud, was the spin of "denial of equal access to
education." Indeed, this issue was raised again and again
each time a student made some threatening remark or act
of defiance and was referred to the office. The "activists"
figured out early that the best way to circumvent
consequences for outrageous or dangerous behavior was
to cut the teacher off at the legs by such contentions. After
all, according to their logic, if the student is spending more
time out of class through disciplinary measures, then how
could there be any learning going on?!

        Dr. Mahmud was quick to use this angle in her
negative evaluations. At one point, I had to bring my
UTLA rep to emphasize that threatening behavior and
violence in class couldn't be condoned, and that there
could be no "educational process" unless there was
cooperation to maintain a normal learning environment.
The parent was presented a one-page detailed report
of logged phone calls with various family members,
documenting reasons for referrals for threats and
subordination. The use of the "f" word and an instance
of stabbing another student with a pencil were among
the most serious. My UTLA rep made the point that her
grade shouldn't have come as a shock to the parent since
other low grades were recorded from other teachers. The
day the student was removed from class for flagrantly
wandering around the room bothering other students, I
was given an example of "Dorsey-style consequences."
No sooner had the student been referred by me to the
Dean, then she returned to the class, accompanied by an
irate "Parent Center" representative, screaming about my
unfair treatment of Blacks. All this took place in front
of my class! Never mind that this was totally illegal and
a security issue. It was being permitted with the tacit
understanding of Dr. Mahmud – and it became a pattern

that could be traced throughout my stay at Dorsey.

During this same conference, a summary of the Administration's observations and recommendations was brought forth: No mentions whatsoever about egregious and outrageous behavior, yet there was a demand that the student henceforth not be removed from class! In other words, I was to swallow all her disparaging remarks, rude attitude and disruptive behavior with no further recourse. At the meeting I pleaded with Dr. Mahmud about this free pass for the student and how it would lead to a complete breakdown in classroom decorum. She was immovable. She knew the serious nature of this student's behavior and now was using it as a set-up in order to degrade my status, and ultimately justify my removal from Dorsey, since there was no way I could keep her in class in the event of future violations. This obnoxious form of harassment, based on my "denying students access to the educational process" became another weapon in an arsenal of unmasked discrimination.

The race card, charges of denial to access, claims of personal enmity-- were the mechanism for stifling any engagement of parental and student accountability at Dorsey. The teacher's union knew what was happening to me, and did nothing. I received many a handshake from my rep, condolences, expressions of regret, wishing they could do more-- otherwise wimpy and lame responses on their part for total impotence.

During my grievance of Dr. Mahmud's negative evaluation, I had invited a different community activist and a personal friend, Reverend Jesse Lee Peterson, head of BOND organization, to sit in on the hearing with the Assistant Superintendent of Schools. At one point, the allegations in the form of letters by community "activists" about the "danger" I represented to the students and their community became so outrageous, that the Reverend stood up, exclaiming, "Mahmud is an outright racist! Mr. Shifren will never get fair treatment from her."

Reverend Peterson made it clear to me: a Black administrator will never rule against another Black colleague in favor of a White teacher. This is the nature of the system in L.A. schools. This is the phenomenon that is palpable and measurable. What's really an eye opener is how overt this type of corruption is-- it's almost embarrassing. No amount of proof otherwise could sway the arbiters of my case that here was an obvious and outrageous case of Black/White discrimination. Letters on my behalf by several District administrators, testimonials by literally all the counseling staff at Dorsey, dozens of positive observations of my classroom management and teaching skills made not the slightest difference in the rush to judgment against me. What was it that topped the scale in ordering my dismissal? The community "activists'" letter about my being a danger to the community and my teaching Hebrew! During the grievance procedure that followed, I had no doubt that this "smoking gun" of a kangaroo court would be so obvious to other investigators that would be taking a closer look at my case. Something so obvious certainly would turn the tide. After all, why was it that I received so many favorable reports in years past, but only in Dorsey was I deemed unfit? What had changed?

The general rule for ruining someone's career is to make an evaluation that has several or even one positive element so as to make the overall picture appear negative. Mahmud's evaluation of me was "unsatisfactory" in ALL categories. Not ONE aspect of my teaching was judged as even being acceptable. Is there such a teacher in existence that is so bad that NOTHING is meritorious about their professional demeanor or performance? In the category, for example, evaluating the efficacy of a teacher's ability to work, and communicate with parents in increasing academic achievement, I received an "unsatisfactory," this at a time when every counselor at Dorsey praised the great lengths I had undertaken to provide tutorials and monitor homework and quizzes by means of daily progress reports to parents, not to mention phone calls home to parents and arranging classroom parent conferences to discuss issues of concern.

This, in my mind, was certainly something that would mitigate against Mahmud's brazen attempt to ramrod me from the District.

"I've heard that the word from the District is that they just don't want you around-- so they have to get rid of you," my UTLA rep subsequently revealed to me. "The cards are stacked against you-- I feel bad about it."

He felt bad? My life was over, my ability to provide a living for my family was at an end. My entire existence was in order to serve as a role model for others, to motivate, to inspire, and mostly to be a vehicle for others' self esteem and accomplishment. It came crashing down. I wanted desperately to believe, despite many incidents of discrimination (in "minority" schools where diversity was sacrosanct), that being White and Jewish would be no impediment to reaching out to Latino and Black youth. This illusion on my part was dashed often during my 15-year career with LAUSD. But I held out, always keeping in my mind that somehow the message of Dr. King, "…judge by one's character and not by the color of their skin," would serve as an equalizing factor, ultimately in any event.

But what is the real trend here in LA? How does cultural diversity actually manifest itself into equitable treatment and fairness in all school matters? A hint at this new agenda can be gleaned from the manifesto drawn up by students and community activists in the wake of the Santa Monica High School riots in the Spring of 2005.

"The Board of Education will ensure that

administration, staff, and faculty hiring practices reflect
the diversity of the student body. Increase outreach and
recruitment of faculty of color who can relate to students'
background and life experiences..."

Well, this conforms neatly with Dr.Mahmud's
agenda and her contention, after my classroom was burned
to the ground, that I'm not "relating" to the students. What
she really meant to say is that my skin color and religion
don't relate to the students. No matter how it hurts to say
it, the pervasive victimization and feeling of being ripped
off by the White man, lurked behind every attempt of
communication and outreach in my years at inner city
schools. The manifesto mentioned above should be a
wake-up call to America. We are grooming a youth that
is expecting their mentors and educators to be cut in the
same mold as the demands of the community "activists."
Diversity really means racism. It's a code word, as much
as we hate to concede the fact. What translates out of
this agenda is that if my son is White, then only a White
man will be ALLOWED to "relate" to him. All values,
morals, and academic wealth of the teacher are first
put to the litmus test of skin color. Hence, the ultimate
institutionalized racism-- passing itself off as progressive.

And what of the disproportionate number of Jews
in high administrative positions with the District and
UTLA? How do they see this new agenda?

LAUSD has a "look-out-for-your-own" model
in dealing with interracial issues and dividing up the tax
dollars for education. It will be determined how many
millions will be spent on "diversity" training during staff
developments, which groups will get what dollars for
programs dealing with ethnic pride, how much money
will be doled out to non-English agendas, etc. Each ethnic
group has its own fiefdom, and absolute discipline is
wielded by their promoters. Except one: the Jews. Look
at our school calendar and find the Jewish holiday, Yom

Kippur, or Day of Atonement, the absolute most solemn and profound expression of this faith. You'll find it listed as an "administrative holiday." No one knows what this date means. From teachers, especially students, you'll come up with a response like, "I guess it's a day off." Any other ethnicity in the city celebrates its sacred or national holidays with pride, festivities, and lots of publicity. LAUSD makes efforts to allot at least some time to the understanding of, for example, Halloween, a completely paganistic ritual, holy to no one.

Why have Jews renounced their heritage and ethnic pride? Drunk with notions of Marxism, One-World-Order, and concepts such as the State being the supreme power, they have run pell mell opposing the present trends of ethnocentrism. A fair amount of guilt about being "chosen" has certainly figured into this equation. The Melting Pot is a Jewish notion, nobody else's. It took one generation of Jewish immigrants to decimate any link to the "old country," erasing Yiddish as a spoken language along with customs of family purity and dietary laws. LAUSD has mandated ethnic foods being available in the cafeteria for years. No Jewish foods here. Black and Latino clothing, hair styles, slang and different schemes for ethnic awareness are rife within the District. You'll not find one aspect of campus life relating to anything that represents a Jewish presence on campus.

Yet, a closer look at UTLA presence on campus shows that Jews are disproportionately represented. In which way does this formidable juggernaut, which takes no small share in molding ideology and agenda in the District, manifest? The Jewish agenda and coexistence with all "progressive" groups, like Gays, Lesbians, Transsexuals, Mecha, Aztlan, bi-lingualism-- in short, all groups that are anethema to traditional Jewish values-- are taken for granted. It would not be an overstatement to say that Jewish identity and ethnic awareness in LAUSD

have been highjacked by a Leftist cabal, bulldozing any
element of sanctity or recognition of a Higher Power in
the face of a youth weaned on massive materialism, media
stranglehold, and pervasive Nihilsm.

At every turn in my career in the District, I
was confronted with these destroyers of everything I
believe in. I may as well have been a Martian, landing on
Earth in a futuristic spacecraft, each time I had a parent
conference with some indignant parent. My outmoded
appearance--head covering, fringes, and long beard-
- seemed to stir up old prejudices as much as shock. A
process of marginalization occurred with the passage
of time. Colleagues were reluctant to bond with my
anachronistic visage, a seeming in-your-face threat to
Western progressive values. Not that I ever considered
myself a victim. Far from it. But, who would be "looking
after me?" Who would rush to justice in the face of death
threats, abusive language, assaults by students, and defiant
behavior by students? The answer of course, is nobody.
So when it becomes time for my conference with a parent
whose son threatened to kill me, Dr. Mahmud could use
the language: "Frankly, Mr. Shifren, it's your word against
his," with impunity. No further concern of any indignant
ethnic group about my rights and sensitivities being
trampled upon could be expected. My position, essentially,
was one of total isolation, marginalization-- in my own
classroom. Of course, there were colleagues with whom I
shared an amicable relationship. But this was superficial
and in no way a measure of any concrete support in the
face of corruption and racism.

Dr. Mahmud entered my class once (early
before school) while I was praying-- prayer shawl and
phylacteries were draped over me. A look of astonishment
and discomfort came across her face. Here was someone
praying to G-d, actually addressing a "higher power"-- a
Jew who actively identified with the ancient ethics of his

Fathers. It was clear that my presence was difficult for her as I was transcending a world beyond the reality of Dorsey's corruption and racism, a world of truth where appellatives of "Dr." or "rabbi" were meaningless. The gauntlet she had placed before me, the incessant cutting me off at the legs through her endless parent conferences and smoke and mirrors style of obscuring truly dysfunctional attitudes at Dorsey, were in stark contrast to my pursuit of values and standards. This was truly a philosophical war for her, one where no prisoners need be taken.

But years earlier I had occasion to experience her style of dealing with "diversity"-- or rather adversity, at Hamilton High School. I had substituted for a Black teacher known for his activist agenda and eccentric cultural views. There was a ruckus involving several students during a class work assignment. One of the most audacious of the students yelled out to me, as I motioned toward them to keep it down, "Hitler should have finished you guys off!"

The student was referred to the assistant principal, who was Dr. Mahmud at that time. I subsequently wrote a report of my version of the events and submitted it to her. Her look of indignation is indelible in my mind to this day: "Do you have a problem with that?" was her shocking response. Fate would have it that 10 years later she would again be my supervisor.

The insidious and hurtful problem with racism is that there is never some clear-cut evidence to root it out. It is now pay-back time for me to be on the receiving end. In the sum of events, who will now hear the call of a white, Jewish man, falling in the abyss of LAUSD? For years I had speculated: Was it a former Jewish boss that had it out for her? Was it a new Black manifesto that had dictated a role of enmity toward my type? I will never know. One thing is for sure: pointing the finger at others will not solve the problems of the masses of students coming from one-parent (or no parents) households, where there is no clear presence of a father figure who instills values. No amount of race-baiting can erase a culture of low self-esteem, a lowering and dumbing down of academic expectations tailor-made by the very minority administrators called to inculcate achievement and adhere to the highest moral and academic standards.

One of my students, Manuel, was on the football team at Dorsey and a real character. He gave me as much of a run for my money as any other disciplinary problem I had had. Nearly a year passed after my removal from Dorsey when I unexpectedly ran into him working at a neighborhood store. We reminisced together and in a totally unsolicited, lengthy exchange, he recounted a meeting with Dr. Mahmud in which she had broken down into tears in her office.

Manual was a student activist, if you could use the term. A leading Chicano spokesman and troublemaker on campus, he was at the forefront of demanding that change be instituted at Dorsey regarding racial incitement and relations. At one point, the Chicano demonstration on campus that he initiated turned violent, with some property damage, students running amok and boycotting classes. Police were called on campus in force, something that is not relished by the administration since this negative attention is a setback for political promotion within the District.

In between sobs, amidst the rioting, Dr. Mahmud was begging Manual to "call off" the Latino students and cease the campus disruptions. This reflects the fundamental, corrupted attitude at Dorsey. There is never a cleaning house, really getting to the problems at hand, rather obfuscation and posturing, a striving for a superficial situation based on appearances, a laissez faire attitude as long as the Administration is not put in a negative light. Black and Latino gangs and others had been at odds for years at Dorsey while a slumbering leadership had allowed problems to fester. Actually it would be incorrect to say that these were sins of omission. Rather, an ultimate form of racism was occurring where Blacks and Latino standards were purposely allowed to be degraded in order not to bring to light a massive failure by the school leadership. The students, however, feel the pressure only in the end of their stay at Dorsey when it becomes clear that their failures in academia now must be reckoned with. A rising, uncontrollable frustration reaches the boiling point when students do not have the grades to graduate, are forced to go to summer school, and have possible sports scholarships in jeopardy. There is heavy pressure, on all sides, with most of the finger-pointing being directed at the teacher.

Several years ago we had a different kind of riot at Dorsey with the main culprit being the California Exit Exam. For several hours, riots were raging, with students being chased by police and a total lockdown was declared. No one was allowed to leave the classroom-- for hours-- for any reason. I called the office asking for permission to permit several students to leave for the restroom.

"Let them pee on the floor," our secretary shot back. I had them leave the class and remain in the building so they could urinate outside my classroom.

The California Exit Exam was proposed by lawmakers to provide some sort of accountability and standardization of statewide levels of competence. Minimum standards were being demanded before students were to receive their diplomas. Of course, this met with student outrage since they knew from the outset that they were not prepared to show basic understanding in the core subjects. They had grown accustomed to being jerked around by phony grading schemes and go-nowhere programs designed to raise grades. Woven into the fraud of the supposed curriculum is the stench of a lowering of expectations spiced up with gimmicks and window dressing to keep the kids unfocused until it's too late.

Dr. Mahmud would in no way go to war with the Black and Latino community, getting at the bottom of the foggy thinking and social malaise that is so pervasive at Dorsey. There would never be an ultimatum leveled at the student body, laced with consequences for violence toward teachers, threatening or abusive discourse, and low levels of behavior and ethics; to do this is to admit a total breakdown in the very reason for Dorsey's existence as an institution. These were the cause of the bitter tears cried by Dr. Mahmud before my student, Manual.

Recently there has been another push by politicians to pass a huge bond issue for Los Angeles schools to the sum of several billion dollars. The answer to poor academic performance is throwing more money at the problem. We are told that in a high tech era there can be no substitute for modern equipment and methods. But who is the politician that will point out how school budgets that were a fraction of the present produced greater results? Peoples' memories fade so as we seemingly grope around in the dark for panaceas to our present quagmire, the path of least resistance is always taken. Additionally, we are told, we must build new schools to keep up with the pace of so many new students entering the District each year.

Several years ago, I taught at Sereno Middle School. One of my students, a Latino, was becoming a severe problem to the extent that his behavior had severely impacted learning. When it became clear at the mid-semester evaluation that he would not pass my class, he reported to the principal that I had threatened to shoot him with a shotgun! This would be laughable if it were true. But the bitter truth was that, as the principal, Mr. Moreno pointed out to me in his office that day, special "terrorism laws" required that I be removed from my position until the allegations could be investigated. Aside from the fact that during the "investigation" I would be laid off without pay, the most egregious factor at play here was that the student's family was here illegally! My life and ability to support my family had been jeopardized by an illegal alien, with the backing of the District.

No amount of overstatement can be used to describe the absolute anarchy in our schools from masses of foreign students, principally from Mexico, that are tying our hands with a myriad of programs designed to bring them up to speed with their grade level. Bi-lingual education is as much a failure as it is a fraud. In nearly all cases, the families are here for economic reasons that have nothing to do with assimilation into American society. Chicano activists abound, and are there to encourage the flood across the border. Groups like Aztlan and Mecha literally preach to these illegals that really it is WE, the White establishment that owes them free education, housing, and a host of other gratuities. Actually, they are told, the "reconquista" (reconquering of Southwest United States) is in full swing, so efforts to learn the host language and culture are unnecessary. Furthermore, since our country has an institutional racism (their claim) toward Latinos, they can only use confrontational politics in attempting to wrest control from the controlling population.

There are no shortage of Leftist groups and sympathizers on hand to help them reach their goal. The Balkanization of our schools is already a fact. Listen to the daily announcements after the morning tardy bell. They are always followed by Spanish and possibly other languages. Whole cadres of teachers and administrators have vested interests in perpetuating this situation. I was once of them. Fluent in Spanish, I would often find myself teaching a bi-lingual class and doing simultaneous translations for foreign students.

But the attitudes and issues mentioned have been

long considered as simply business as usual. No one
questions the fact that people are already burgeoned with
their own learning disabilities. The system is imploding
from sheer numbers. Those whose agenda it is to destroy
our country from within, are aided and abetted by the
Administration's laissez faire policy toward aliens.
Their presence serves a higher purpose. Since "cultural
diversity" has been taken up as the new mantra of the
Left, the logical consequence is that our own American
institutions based on G-d, patriotism, individual rights and
freedoms guaranteed by our constitution, have suddenly
come into question. The illegal alien agenda is one of
the weapons used in a vast arsenal to break our system.
A new moral relativism has replaced common sense
and patriotic civic awareness. After all, the logic of the
destroyers and haters of Christianity and America goes, if
we can nurture and promote Latino pride, bi-lingualism,
and cultural diversity aggressively enough, then the whole
premise of America can be brought into question. The
more Third World, non-English speaking people flooding
through our schools, the better (they believe). The proof
that this agenda is working can be seen in the District's
policy of not questioning legal residence status of any
foreigners. There are gangs in our schools, terrorizing
entire communities, whose members are here illegally. A
little-known fact is that nearly one third of California state
prison inmates are illegal aliens.

     This is the choke hold that has to a large degree
impeded academic achievement and access to educational
resources in many of our schools. At any given time, when
the opportunity becomes convenient, a hue and cry of
"racism" is heard by Latino activists when their agenda is
questioned. Really, how am I as a teacher, to discipline or
fairly evaluate a child when the specter of the race card is
played out at regular intervals? The problem, of course,
is exacerbated by weak-kneed administrators who simply
want to coast along to their pensions without any attention

focused on them, so the situation festers and becomes out
of control-- hopefully on someone else's watch.

Recently, I attended a community meeting
where L.A. City Councilman Bernard Parks and LAUSD
Assistant Superintendent Alonzo spoke. Both were in
complete denial about the invasion of illegal aliens in
our schools and communities, using instead flowery
explanations about the need to "get along" and have
"compassion" for diverse ethnicities. Parks pointed out
that instead of focusing on who is not here legally, we
need to create a better economic climate in the city,
create more affordable housing and foster understanding.
Both men were roundly criticized and taken to task for
the corrupted thinking that has helped impoverish our
schools and cheapen the standard of education. But more
important, how has the leadership so failed us? If this
is the level of decay in our body politic on top, how is
the classroom teacher expected to deal with the malaise
caused by the destroyers from within? The answer is, he
reconciles with the corruption and becomes a part of it-- or
he is terminated for upholding academic standards and
appropriate levels of classroom decorum.

For this reason, Dorsey had a turnover rate of
its teaching faculty of nearly one third on a yearly basis.
Their method was as insidious as it was effective: new
teachers were recruited yearly to replace the burnt out staff
that simply had to go elsewhere. The new teachers were
pliable and submissive, many with emergency credentials
who could ill afford to draw appropriate conclusions about
the corrosive effects of the corruption upon classroom
integrity. By the time they figured out the system,
predictable indifference and cynicism became so ingrained
that they themselves had become an integral part of the
overall malaise.

One of our students was shot and killed by a
fellow student. The reason? He refused to turn over his

cool-looking Converse high top sneakers to the punk who demanded them. So he was shot to death, his sneakers taken, and the whole community was in an uproar. District "psychologists" were rushed to the school to deal with the stress and taut nerves on campus. Several days of dialog were held. I was amazed at the reactions of many in my class, often bordering on indifference and a "whatever" attitude.

"Don't you realize what's happened here?" I excitedly remarked after I saw where our dialog was headed. "One of your classmates was just killed over a lousy pair of shoes!"

My distraught mood wasn't shared by the students. A pathetic level of disinterest was palpable during our exchange. "That's just how it is, you can't change things," one of our female students confided. Funny, later on I took one of my better students aside and wanted to know what's up with the insane reactions.

"Oh, they don't want to say nuthin' cuz some homies might take revenge and jump them."

A total lack of leadership and reluctance to insist on values and a proper code of conduct has led to the present situation where the gangs have become stakeholders in communities, forcing their toxic concoction of violence and nihilism down the throats of fellow students. Not long ago, several disruptive students were to be transferred from Jefferson to Washington High. One of the counselors became aware that the transfer could not be implemented since the students (Crips gangmembers) would be threatened by the Bloods at that school! District policymakers and educators are now being held hostage by the punks! But the public, too busy making a living to pay the fat salaries of these psychotic "administrators," is clueless about the extent of the corruption.

Each one of us growing up in America remembers the Pledge of Allegiance. This small act did more than anything to unify the diverse mosaic of cultures and ethnic groups. We instinctively knew that we were bound together through a higher purpose, with a spiritual and patriotic calling. Later each of us was aroused by President Kennedy's plea that we ask not what our country can do for us but rather what we can do for it. And I remember the bitter tears we shed when he fell. It was like the heavens had fallen. Altruism, civic responsibility, love of G-d and country (dare I add respect for teachers and authority!)-- these weren't just abstract philosophies. How well we remember our report cards of old, with grades in "civics" and "citizenship." The flag, the country, its institutions and values-- these all coalesced to give purpose to our lives.

My class at Dorsey had no flag, despite requests to get one. No pledge of allegiance here. Nothing spiritual or patriotic was presented to give the faintest hint of something more profound than "it's all about me." Nothing but victimization, finger pointing, race baiting-- somehow the problem is over there-- those "folks in the other neighborhoods"-- never did anything occur that was a direct result of my own lack of citizenship, respect for teacher and school, my lack of cooperation in completing assignments and keeping up with class standards. In such a vacuous, dumbing down system replete with apologists and malevolent educators, is it any wonder how a student could get blown away simply because his fellow student coveted his sneakers?

I received a letter one day in my mailbox from a student who had been absent for nearly a month. "Dear Mr. Shifren, I apologize for not letting you know that I would miss taking your final exam. I was on my way to school when I got shot. I should do OK. Thanks for letting me take the test when I get back."

Shot on the way to school? The guy pulled the

trigger was not some rabid Klansman or other anti-Black xenophobe. He was a member of the community and definitely Black. He just "thought" my student was a rival gang member. Where's the outrage by Dr. Mahmud about my student, about a situation where American children have no higher calling in life other than exacting revenge for perceived gang affiliation. This is the miserable harvest we've reaped as a result of our corrupted school system. There is a battery of lawyers out there ready to litigate against G-d, the flag, and love of country, but where are they when teachers and students are threatened or shot?

We are drowning in our own political correctness. On December 7 one year, I asked the principal why there was no mention of the attack on Pearl Harbor. "Oh, we don't want to offend or be judgmental toward students of Asian heritage," was her inane excuse. But of course, if having a flag in class was in issue, then what could be expected of remembering an essential moment in our country's history?

I recall during our final exams a group of students hell-bent on disrupting the class. One student insisted on getting out of his seat and wandering around class, chatting with friends. This, despite clear written instructions that any talking would be grounds for failing the test. These students "dropped by" on finals day after a four-month absence. No absence note, nothing from parents explaining what was going on, simply came by to see old buddies on the last day of school. Threats were made against me, foul language used; I then called for campus police to remove them.

What I will never forget is Mrs. Webb, our assistant principal, saying to the biggest rowdy: "Come on baby, come with me…"

Baby?! He was 6'3", weighed at least 230 pounds for crying out loud! This was a typical attitude at Dorsey, treating the kids as victims, somehow downtrodden innocents, leaving the subtle inference that it is the TEACHER who is using his authority in an unwarranted manner. Throw in the usual refrain of "lack of sensitivity to minority students" and you get the big picture.

The constant, affectionate use of the term "baby" during our innumerable parent conferences was an effort to blunt documented referrals for disruptive behavior and disrespect toward the teacher or students. Mrs. Webb's patronizing to students and parents during those humiliating meetings was designed to wear down my ability to effectively manage my class and uphold high (or at least normal) standards of conduct. This cutting-the-teacher-off-at-the-legs tactic put students on notice that rudeness, lack of preparation and failure to bring pencil, pen, paper, books, and assorted examples of disruption could definitely continue and would be condoned by the administration.

At any given moment at Dorsey, you could hear the cracking of 2-way radios blaring. It was always a source of humor and curiosity to hear who was being busted and where. A typical transmission:

"Base to 15, students are reporting throwing objects of paper into Mr. Shifren's class, please check it out."

"15 to base, at the scene, no students are there."

Every hallway, every area of senior and junior quad, football field, track, parking lot, cafeteria, is patrolled by campus "security," with their ubiquitous walkie-talkies. Every administrator carries one as well. Between the expenses of the communications labyrinth, security staff, campus police, deans and other auxiliary staff indirectly involved, the District pays well over one-half million dollars yearly. More precious time is wasted herding the hundreds of tardy students to classes daily.

Mr. Ausbon, a former football coach at Hamilton High, could be heard every morning excoriating the minions of late-comers as they were lined up for the daily "tardy sweep." The hundreds of students cornered from all areas of the campus would be corralled at the cafeteria where they'd be issued tardy slips to get them back to class. Mr. Ausbon's bellowing voice (which could be heard from all points of the campus), admonishing the students about the connection between punctuality and their financial futures, was a daily mantra that went nowhere. The same kids would filter into class, each with his or her tardy slip in hand, causing more wasted time while distracting the already hard-to-focus class. I can think of nothing more aggravating to a teacher than having to interrupt a lesson to deal with a constant stream of late students, each with his own snicker on his face, acknowledging a perfectly torpedoed lesson. It was safe to say that the five to ten percent rate of overall campus tardiness had a tremendous impact on the school as well as the high rate of failures.

The question is: Why were these students allowed to chronically disturb classes with their late arrivals. The administration knew who they were, yet nothing was done about it. These same students were the most at-risk of failing, of adding to our legions of unemployable youth as a result of poor organizational and academic skills. It would not be an overstatement that failing to rein in these kids before the negative patterns developed, contributed to a general breakdown in the community and further burdened the social welfare and criminal justice system, locally and elsewhere. And why? Because it's not easy to insist on superior conduct and academic performance-- an all-out effort would accentuate "racial tensions" and exacerbate already low self-esteem, as it were, of many of the student body. So Dr. Mahmud, at some point, realized that she'd be moving on, climbing through the intractable District hierarchy, leaving behind her indelible mark on the school. Indeed, two years after her arrival at Dorsey, she was promoted. Her "fiddling-while-Dorsey-burns" attitude (in this case, quite literally) was not lost on the students, and its impact on the teachers was palpable, if uncontested and unmentioned.

Ironically, I had occasion to bump into a former Dorsey student while I held a position as a teacher in a rehab program at Peter Pitchess Honor Ranch, one of the detention centers of L.A. County. One of the Black inmates asked me if I'd help him fill out forms needed to process those entering the jail. As I watched this pitiful individual struggle with basic vocabulary, I noticed tears well up in his eyes.

"Mr. Shifren, they never taught me nuthin," he sobbed, staring blankly at the forms. "If they woulda taught me to read, I wouldn't be here now."

Who knows what was up with him? But one thing was certain: He attended Dorsey and left not knowing how to read. His actions, as a result of his unemployability, resulted in incarceration, damage to others or property, and cost tax payers $30,000 yearly.

All this because of an administration bent on political correctness, using the time-honored business-as-usual obfuscation already infamous in the District.

Learning is difficult. It requires diligence, perseverance, and self-sacrifice. More importantly in this era of expected instant results, it requires deferred gratification. Failure is a big part of achievement. Knowing what we're deficient in and why we're not measuring up to high standards, is sometimes as important as reaching the goal itself. One of the great advantages of individual sports is that a person is confronted with personal weakness and that overcoming this is the measure of attained achievement. No one can be blamed, no excuses can be used for not reaching the mark. What makes teaching

so rewarding is the opportunity to spur on the student
to overcome weakness, to motivate them in rising to the
expected outcome and even beyond. There is nothing more
satisfying than hearing from a student years later how
we as educators had served to jumpstart their entry into
critical, free-thinking and self-discipline.

     In this spirit, I had always considered my role at
Dorsey akin to a coach-- at times remonstrating, cajoling,
encouraging students to go the extra mile, extending
beyond their present capabilities. Learning Spanish was
the job of my charges; however, my task went beyond
the verbs and vocabulary into the sphere of outstanding
study skills and responsibilities. More often than not, my
students, I had hoped, would remember me not for their
competence in a foreign language, but rather the attitude
gained necessary to be a winner, to experience the feeling
of working hard and the satisfaction of knowing that they
had done the task required-- without lowering the bar.

     The understanding and appreciation of this
serious approach to learning could only be realized in an
environment where learning FOR ITS OWN SAKE had
merit. The pursuit of knowledge, unfettered by apologetics
and victimization, demanded that the leadership be of one
mind in this goal. My credibility at Dorsey was only as
good as Dr. Mahmud's support of academic excellence,
discipline, and the highest of classroom standards. The
REAL racism at Dorsey occurred when she informed me
that I had to "back off from being so harsh." Indeed, the
"harshness" I exhibited in classroom management centered
around respect for others, punctuality, and being prepared
to study with pen, paper, and book. Short of this, there
would certainly be "harsh" consequences. And this was
the whole issue. One couldn't very well expect inner-city,
Black students to toe the line, went the thinking. It was
"unreasonable" to expect Black kids to not use the "F"
word on penalty of being thrown out of my class. The true

racism at Dorsey was allowing students to chronically
come to class late, to get away with not doing homework,
and for calling in disgruntled parents to discuss failures,
inferring that the teacher is somehow out of sync with the
prevailing torpor and sloth in dispensing of grades.

Everything was played out, predictably as
clockwork, to cultivate an atmosphere of revelry,
slothenliness, and hysteric lack of accountability. In
the two years I spent at Dorsey, not once did I hear the
principal chide students for poor performance and lack of
self-control. Countless hours were spent in dealing with
horseplay in the hallways, marauding students whimsically
roaming the campus in search of thrills, girlfriends-
- something, but anything other than what was taking
place in class. Yet not once was this issue attacked head
on. Never was there any attempt to mete out draconian
consequences for verbally or physically abusing teachers.

How the tune changed, and with it the pretense
of solemnity, each Martin Luther King day. Gone
was the pompous, asinine attitude on the part of the
administration. The foolishness and demeaning elements
of staff development changed to a heightened awareness-
- a new sense of victimization. How I wish that Dr. King
would have visited my classes, observed first hand the
out-of-control attitudes and insane behaviors. Would
that he had heard the whining and bellyaching from the
"overburdened" students, the excuses for being months
late on term papers, the half-baked rationale about why
assignments were not typed or contained so many errors
as to render them inadmissible. Oh, how I had wished for
a TRUE appreciation of what he gave his life for-- instead
of the miasma of gang-related shootings, "in-the-hood"
consciousness, the filth and debauchery of the Dorsey
pop-culture-- all wrapped up neatly and packaged by the
racist administration as "diversity" in giving homage to
Dr.King's memory.

Dare a mention of the catch word "diversity"
be made on Dr. King's birthday? What about judging
each man by his character and not the color of his skin?
Does this really apply to a white, a Jew? Does diversity
appreciation include non-Hispanics, non-Blacks?

We are poised on the edge of civilization, having
reached a point-of-no-return in our survival as a nation.
The freedoms that have made us the greatest nation on
Earth are being challenged by new, alien philosophies.
As of this writing, it is a given that our nation will suffer
another 9/11 type attack, possibly many more times
devastating than the first. How will we survive-- not just
physically-- but endure the mayhem and social upheaval
to come? What will be the types of values that will give us
the inner fortitude and courage to resist and vanquish an
enemy bent on destroying us?

The destroyers from within are also poised to serve
as a vanguard for the coming attack. But they come not
bearing arms. Their sedition and betrayal takes the form of
a culture war, being waged right now, in our schools. The
sapping of the will to resist tyranny and oppression must
begin in our schools.

The most insidious shot over the bow in the
culture war, preceding the real war that our country must
survive, is the notion of diversity. No one who entered
Ellis Island starting with waves of immigration ever
entertained the thought of "diversity." Each immigrant ran
as fast as possible from a European mind set to become
an American. Language and culture were united in the
schools across the land. There was no "English-as-a-
second-language." My mother sat in a class in Queens,
N.Y., with Italians, Irish, Slovaks, and others. No Yiddish
was used in translations. There was common acceptance
that a total and complete immersion into American
language and culture, during school hours, was the key
to unifying the people. Without this philosophy, America

would become the Europe they had left behind.

The "one-world-order" we hear about, so ubiquitously bantered about in the media, is already alive and well in our schools. The proponents of "diversity" understand that by accentuating our differences and mandating dispensations for them, they can effect a corrosion of that nationalistic glue that holds us together. The supplanting of the message of the Forefathers and founders of the nation with the insipid values of those seeking to divide us is key to the brainwashing of our youth.

I don't recall, in all my years of teaching, the articulating of national pride and altruism for the sake of our country. The opposite has been the case. Radicals have been allowed to bend the minds of our students, and opposing their positions considered tantamount to Right-wing facism. It is completely in vogue to tout seditious rhetoric in the schools, without an afterthought of the damage it causes.

Those serving the cause of our national debauchery are right on track with their dissemination of the new sexuality and its mores. Suddenly, homosexual and lesbian "rights"-- along with those of the transgender and transdressers-- are of import. Suddenly our students' levels of achievement and measure of civic responsibility must now compete with philosophies that are alien to the values of family and the spirit. Taking a look at the Communist Manifesto, it becomes clear that an essential element in breaking the will of the people before taking them over, is the instituting of sexual depravity and relativism. Once a nation is morally confused, it can then accept every dogma in a relativistic sense, thereby giving a stamp of approval to the very philosophies designed to undermine our country. Ultimately, we will live with Good that is Evil, and Evil that is Good.

The "diversity" proponents understand that ultimately all expressions of sanctity for a Higher Being need to be attacked and neutralized. Much like the generation of the Tower of Babel, it is imperative to destroy the country's will by going straight to its source of righteousness. The greatest Jewish leader in modern time, the Lubavitcher Rebbe, was once asked what was the secret of the strength of America. His answer was well known to America's detractors and destroyers: A firm religious foundation and a belief in G-d. He never mentioned individual faiths or paths of worship.

The alienation of our youth from the military started with the Peace Movement on the campuses during the 60's. We have evolved to the point where ROTC on campus is somehow considered anti-peace and war mongering. For centuries, it was a part of an American child's life to be surrounded by guns. Cars and pick-ups with gun racks were seen across the land. It would never occur to anyone to kill another human being over a pair of tennis shoes, for example. An awe and respect for firearms and their proper care was standard. Nor has this country seen the level of filth and violence through the media and its diabolic array of video games run amok. Parents are at their wits end to somehow censor the incessant amounts of gratuitous violence and simulated kill modules. The hypocrisy of the new order on the campuses, presently raising their corrupted voices in demanding a removal of symbols of military violence from campuses cries out to the heavens. Instead, we're left to collectively shake our heads about the phenomena such as Columbine and other violent outrage in the schools.

I remember several occasions at Dorsey when we were locked down as a result of suspected weapons on campus, with LAPD swat teams and dogs patrolling the campus. The interruption of classes by the jarring, prying open and slamming shut of lockers in search for guns and knives was certainly more provocative than any military presence on campus. The frequent occurrences of shootings in the community by gang members was sloughed off by the Administration as water off a duck's back. No, only when the military is portrayed with guns do we get riled up. The fact that the punks and gangbangers are walking around with automatic Uzis and 9mm's is not a problem.

Therefore, the anti-military hysteria by the new order on campus can actually be seen in a larger sense as a desensitization of our youth toward a natural instinct to self-preservation, deferring instead to a Big Brother government which is empowered with our protection. Indeed, never had I heard any discussion of the value of the Second Amendment and its impact on a free society. The enemy from within understands that the usurping of a sense of the people's right and will toward self-defense is a natural step in a one-world type takeover.

But if military symbolism with its firepower is considered so repulsive by the Leftist administrators, why is there no outrage when our own kids are plugging each other or stabbing each other? The answer is the racist view of these administrators that it's OK for Blacks and Hispanics to carry heat, just not Whites. After all, these punks and hoodlums with their indiscriminate killings of innocents in the community, are simply lashing out at the institutional White racism so pervasive in our society, so goes the thinking. And seen from this jaded view, the kid that threatened to kill me was really doing the right thing. Certainly, there was nothing egregious about wanting to kill me: after all, I'm White, and a Jew to boot. Confirmation of this was acknowledged by Dr. Mahmud herself, when she noted that a threat on my life was nothing more than an every day occurrence: "It happens in politics all the time," in her own words.

Our attitudes and responses in condoning and

tacitly validating the hideous violence portrayed in our popular culture are driving our youth to the brink. When a community at Dorsey can be moved to write a letter to the District about how I am a "destructive" influence upon their students and at the same time remain silent about the raging gang wars over drugs and turf-- we're talking about a dangerous denial that will threaten our entire society.

It already has. Over one percent of our entire U.S. population is incarcerated. The majority are Black. I think every educator would do well to tour the prisons popping up across the land. As they say, "It's a whole new world." During my stay as a teacher to inmates at the L.A. County jail in Castaic, I was amazed at the racism between Black and Latino prisoners. Once I was to monitor the mopping up of a particular cell. I noticed that nothing was happening, despite instructions given concerning the clean-up. Then a prisoner approached me.

"Mr. Shifren, ain't nuthin' gonna happen here unless you separate 'em," was the oblique report.

"What do you mean?" I asked naively.

"No brothers gonna work with Mexicans. They gotta stay separated or else they'll start a riot."

So much for the billions wasted on multi-culturalism. In our classrooms, Blacks and Hispanics regularly sat separate. If I wanted to "punish" one of the guys for being a loudmouth, I'd simply stick a Brother next to a Hispanic, or vice versa. It was the best classroom management I ever performed...

My supervisor had to remove one of my students (a Black), a disciple of the Nation of Islam, who wrote the prison warden: "I am requesting to be removed from Mr. Shifren's class. If I remain, I take no responsibility for any injury I might cause him. His race is despicable and a blemish upon all Muslims and I am sworn to do him physical harm."

     I delayed writing this book for over a year. There were several reasons: Bitterness and revulsion in picking up a pen and recording my thoughts of how I was literally run out of the District, kept me away. Like any other person that has experienced institutionalized prejudice, there is a deep seated anger mixed with an awesome feeling of impotence, effectively pushing away our desire to act for a change. The system that cast me aside is so pervasive and impenetrable, I felt incapable of confronting any level of its corruption.

     I had seen my hopes for redress dashed again and again in the kangaroo courts they held during my grievance hearings. Over and over, Mahmud and her lawyers simply based their decision to fire me on the poor performances of students and alleged classroom management discrepancies. The ubiquitous stacks of letters from concerned parents were mentioned constantly regarding my lack of sensitivity toward community and students.

     The prison is a reflection of the degradation in the communities I had taught. We spoonfeed the kids a daily pablum of diversity, ethnicity and victimization to justify the lousy scores and make the kids feel good about themselves after all. Some of the prisoners at the jail were simply evil. But many were associated with gangs in the Dorsey environment, gangs that were never confronted with the hard knocks reality of becoming successful in America. Excuses and denial were their reality in failure at their schools; social promotion, saving face, passing them up to the next grade became more of a priority than qualifying the human being for the life skills of reading, writing, and math.

     My individual tragedy can only be mitigated by realizing the ticking time bomb going on in our schools.

There are doubtless scores of other teachers who have been assaulted or threatened and live in a deathly silence, afraid of retaliation and losing their pensions. They prefer to keep the status quo, because they know that there's no redress against a corrupted system. So the terror and racism goes unchallenged. The unions are an accomplice-- they don't want any scrutiny from outsiders, lest they be taken to task for the anarchy in their District.

And then there are the Roy Romer types-- simply fiddling away as the student scores grow worse, and drop-out rates increase, and the City becomes a simmering cauldron of unemployable youth, with no self-esteem except from their "homies" in their gang communities. It will take an act of war for America to realize the extent of the problem. No one has time, and no one can really grasp the warping of the minds of our kids. Far more dangerous to our society, infinitely more insidious than Al Qaida terrorism, is the terrorism that occurs daily in our schools. The toxic combination of diversity teaching on the one hand, and victimization on the other, coupled with the "educators" covering their collective backsides no matter what-- these are the corrosive factors here at home that no foreign power can accomplish.

I have raised an issue for community leaders to deal with. It's my hope that it won't be ignored. There are no more suburbs to escape to. We've made our bed, we'll have to sleep in it. We all will feel the pain of a failing student becoming a parent without survival skills in a technological society, who in desperation will do anything. We keep thinking that more prisons for these kids that got away without doing homework for years is the answer. We keep up the fallacious belief that more cops will somehow protect us against our former students who were fed the mantra that it is the White man bringing them down. We just can't divest ourselves from the myths about the "educational experts" (hardened Leftists and Communists)

providing solutions to caring for our most precious assets-
- our children.

I hope that each person reading my story will reflect
upon their own inaction and perhaps take a lesson in
responsible parenting and guardianship of our local
schools. We need not be experts to grasp that our national
strength has come from a belief in G-d, in the eternal bond
with a Creator that has given us the ability to choose Good
and Righteousness, or its opposite.

Intro to teacher testimonial from Jordan High

I have spent over a year soliciting comments and feedback from former colleagues who have either been terminated or retired from the District for reasons of corruption or racism directed toward them. In no instance have any of these individuals volunteered to share their unfortunate experiences. My department chairman, a twenty-year veteran at Dorsey High, was intimately involved with me at all stages of my stay at Dorsey: from the burning down of my classroom to physical assaults and threats. He declined the offer to give any testimonial on my behalf, despite his having retired from the District. It was explained to me that the memories of his experience at the school had brought back such negative feelings that, despite his willingness to help, he couldn't bring himself to step backwards into that dark period.

There have been other colleagues who are now working at other schools, having managed to make a quiet exit from Dorsey. They feel threatened by retaliatory measures that the District might take against them should they offer any testimonial. Several of my colleagues who have had tenure for twenty-five years or more, have expressed concern that any "stirring up trouble" on their part would impact their pensions.

Personally speaking, it is remarkable the absolute hegemony that the District has over the hearts and minds of so many thinking and enlightened individuals. Worse, of course, is the unbreakable code of silence that keeps the corruption and racism on the back burner.

After the seemingly endless back slaps and high-fives from my colleagues for completing my expose that they themselves were afraid to lend their names to, I was made aware of a teacher who had taught at Jordan High in Watts. She is a teacher's teacher-- full of idealism and dedication-- even in the most challenging situations. It is an honor for me to share her story with you.

A Tale from the Inside

The only job for which I have been interviewed and not hired was a job teaching for Los Angeles Unified School District. I was fresh out of college, dressed to the nines, and proudly ready to extol the virtues of a profession I had wanted to enter since I was in the ninth grade. I shook the Principal's hand and was told not to sit down, that he didn't want to waste my time. He shamelessly told me that I was "too white." According to the Principal, fresh from the fax my name – with all its consonants stuck together – looked minority-like, very hirable. In person, my skin and features were just Teutonic enough to get him in trouble. For the record, he was white and had pointed out that if I were any other color we'd not "be having this conversation," a conversion that I like to refer to as a racist act. On the way out of my failed interview, I stopped to examine a faculty photo, taken the previous year, in which there were no white teachers. So much for the "racial balance" he'd said he was forced to create.

That was five years ago, before teaching jobs outside the district and before my short stint again with LAUSD. I did get hired eventually as a ninth-grade English teacher at Jordan High School in Watts. But that was an easy job to land: I'd taken one of seventeen positions, according to the Vice Principal, that had remained unfilled for two years. The only kind of beating down doors going on at Jordan was the type that gets you out.

For those unfamiliar, the school is smack-dab in the middle of Blood-Crip territory; and while the notorious gangs are known to have made their peace, there is no shortage of other violent gang activity in the area or on Jordan's campus. In fact, most of my fourteen-year-old students were either gang members or in the process of being inducted. I could always spot the newest inductees by the severe, never-tell-why bruises that appeared at least once per week.

The day before I was hired, the Vice Principal made sure that I understood what I would be getting myself into. She walked me around the campus so that I could get a close-up view of students; see how they dress; listen to them talk. She told me about the surrounding projects, which fed the school most of its population, and of a recent on-campus gang fight that had made big network news. Nothing deterred me. I felt comfortable and was up for the challenge; however, going to Jordan for the first time is like seeing the Grand Canyon, sort of: All the photos, articles or rumors don't buffer you from the shock or speechlessness over actually being there. Day after day, the school's culture and goings-on of support staff, administration and other teachers left me stunned.

Hurry up and Wade

Starting my job mid-year, I was anxious to get into the classroom with students who'd not had a regular teacher all year, particularly in light of the fact that the school has such a high drop-out rate, about seventy-five percent, from what I was told, and mostly occurring the second semester of ninth grade. Unfortunately, the students and I had to wait for another three weeks after my hire so that I could complete a week-long training program required by LAUSD, a program booked for two weeks.

There, two retired teachers brushed through information that takes at least a year in any credential program – a waste of time for me, one who'd been through a credential program, and not helpful to those hired under emergency credentials (now euphemistically known now as the District Intern Program). The biggest waste was to students awaiting a regular teacher during a most crucial time. There, too, in the unpaid, though required, crash course, I took away a few unexpected words of wisdom from the teacher vets, my favorite being how to get students you don't like out of your classroom for a day by having them wander the campus in various mapped out places looking for a non-existent can of paint the teacher must say is desperately needed. Seems mean, but that's just me. I'm a teacher, and most teachers I know are kid friendly. But, hey, who can complain? Those taxpayers' dollars were hard at work – LAUSD monies well spent.

Might I add that nothing that week was useful? I had to learn on the job about typical procedure and protocol, and even then, at the school, it was with little support or guidance. I refer now to my first experiences at LAUSD, with all the paper work and so on, as my "Hurry-up-and-Wade" phase of the job, a phase that never ended.

Tag!

Now, kids, "tag" is a noun, a name or an after thought added to the end of a sentence – isn't that right? Oh, yeah, it's also a verb, an action that created that lovely artwork you're sitting on, the stuff all over your desks and on our walls, the stuff all over the dictionaries on the broken down shelf in the back of the room and the old, yellowing posters.

My classroom was littered with tagging, so much of it that there wasn't much room left to tag, so taggers tagged atop of tagging. (New gangs need new, illegible letters, I always say. You gotta represent!).

I might be the most understanding teacher alive when it comes to tagging. It doesn't take a lot of research to know that tagging is symptomatic of not having a voice, of not feeling recognition. I also know how unsympathetic the non-tagging world is, how unproductive tagging is, too, so as much as possible I cleaned and scraped and painted away tagging the weekend before I began teaching, readying myself to teach more powerful methods of gaining attention or effecting change, and readying myself to provide opportunities often to do so. Oddly enough, I was partly blamed by an administrator for the tagging, told that I should keep a better eye on things, even though I wasn't at the school during the artwork sessions.

The tagging was not restricted to the classroom. Students also marked up the hallways, which always smelled of paint. Tagging went up – paint was splattered over. Always there was the smell of wet paint. The empty corridors were so prison-like, so un-school-like, as though the students were being groomed for their future time "inside." Once, as I was leaving my classroom, a few girls were running through the hallway laughing, when another teacher yelled, "Get out of here! Don't make me get the police up here!" We had a police station just below my classroom. Jeez, I miss the good old days when laughing and running after school were at their very worst annoying to grownups.

My building housed several hundred students throughout the day. Thank God we had that one woman who was afraid of the kids monitoring things. The police were usually, understandably, busy about the campus or in their offices, behind their locked doors. Oh, and thank God, too, that we had that one Dean in charge of all the discipline at the school. Why spend money hiring needed people for kids who are just going to drop out or go to prison? Best leave things as is. Blame the teachers for what's wrong then tie their hands as often as possible.

Sorry to digress. Allow me to speak again of my room, and the most important part of it: Besides being prolifically tagged and filthy, many of its chairs were broken, a fact I reported immediately and for many days thereafter, as nothing was being done. Eventually, the administration's solution was to remove all of the chairs.

I brought things into the classroom, so disgusted with the part-alley-way part prison-like environment, so enthused to make it different. With a great looking and stimulating environment and good classroom management, there is still no guarantee students will learn, but it doesn't hurt to try. I had accumulated a lot of things in my short time teaching, which have fallen into some Jordan abyss – I've not gotten them back: my small lending library for the students; my teacher resources; autographed books from authors, including my favorite often used book, an autographed book of poetry for teens, written by Pat Mora, who visited one of my classrooms a few years back; gifts and letters from former students and colleagues (to keep my spirits up – just in case); art and posters galore. I did what I could.

The room was small and hot, too small for a few of my five classes. I never before was happy about truancy, but sometimes that in abundance was the only thing that allowed all of my students to all sit at one time. The room was just big enough, and I mean just big enough, to fit about twenty-five chairs. I actually organized the desks daily to make room wide enough for me to walk down one or two of the rows so that I could check students' work or help them. I rotated. Mondays I did the first few rows, Tuesdays the next few and so on, to be fair to all.

I put students without seats to work, posting, for example, new vocabulary words to the word wall, or alphabetizing papers, or whatever. With twenty-five chairs and thirty-three students in one particular class, I had to get very creative. That was the class chosen by the counseling office for sending new enrollees, daily. I can't recall the number of visits to the counseling office, nice ones too, where I would politely say, "All are welcome, but no more will fit; come visit if you don't believe me, please. It's just fifty feet thatta way." Two words: Brick wall. They just looked at me as though I were speaking a foreign language and continued to send kids.

That too was the class where my RSP teacher (resource specialist, required by law for those with learning disabilities) came to visit, and when I say visit I don't mean a euphemism for actual work. She did nothing. Absolutely nothing.

As a new teacher to the district I wasn't sure how pro-active she or I was to be, together or if together at all, in the planning for our students with special needs, so I asked her. She was the expert. I tried all sorts of things to get her involved. I got nothing but, "Well, let's see how it goes." She was lovely, to tell you the truth, a very nice woman and supportive of me, had a super-great smile, but just couldn't bring herself to do anything but take up space in my already overly crowded room. Adding to matters, when grades were due, she asked me to provide grades for her, grades that she was supposed to have given each of those legally entitled students. No apologies were made, just, "Can I have your grades so I have something to turn in?"

I mentioned this fact to a seemingly kind teacher who was nearby in another classroom, wondering if this were typical. This was his reply: "We are white. We don't matter to those who run things here." This was in reference to my RSP teacher's skin color. She was African American. Now, whether a true fact or not, a non-sequitur to my question or not, the idea that non-black-skinned teachers and staff were treated with less courtesy was shared among many at Jordan, including long-time veterans, and it was shared with me often and early as one of the big, looming truisms of not just Jordan but all of LAUSD. I relate this with a bit of trepidation because not having spent a lot of time at Jordan, I only sensed what I was warned about; it remained an intangible fact for me. Maybe I'm slow to believe what

I witnessed? Still, I'd never heard so much talk of who disliked whom because of skin color, of who didn't receive equal treatment because of skin color. One teacher had said to me, "Watch out for those Black Bitches in the office. You know how Black women can be, shoving their fat asses around." I began to wonder: With racial tension among those who run the school, how would we ever decrease it among students? And how far upstream did this excrement begin its flow downward?

Teacher, Interrupted

I loved the kids instantly, especially a funny Latino male student who constantly reminded me, "Mizz, weez Watts kids, man." I once opened the closet where I kept personal items like my purse; when this student noticed, he'd said, "Mizz, you can't bring that shit here: Weez Watts kids, man." He meant it sincerely to protect me, and he was right. You couldn't leave a grimy, broken pencil unattended if you wanted to keep it. Among other things, I'd actually had a grimy, broken pencil taken from my desk.

Three weeks it took from constantly being known by the students as the "stupid white ho who came to the hood" (no joke) to teacher who was to be protected, at least by some. I worked hard and was consistent. I noticed dramatic change in many of the students, behaviorally, if not academically – and that's where learning begins for students, with their valuing time spent in the classroom. The behavior, I feel, reflected their start of valuing the time they would spend with me. I was told that the administration was leaving me alone to let me get my feet wet but that sooner or later they would begin interrupting classes. They did – interrupt, that is.

Teachers, support staff and administrators began telling me that I must be doing something right. Kids were staying in my class, not being sent to the Dean, not running out of class. When a district person or administrator did visit my class, the kids were on-task and engaged in learning. Those first few weeks left me euphoric, minus a few episodes, minus the swearing at me by students ("who the F' are you, white ho?") and the many times some were up in my face, trying to scare me with close, threatening physical proximity, standing in their territorial stances. I was never frightened, not once (Bully for me...maybe I should have been?). The most threatening students were some of the ones I grew closest to before I left. It nearly made me feel like staying forever. And let me tell you, left to my own devices, left to do my job, all might have worked out like an ending of Dangerous Minds – without the blue jeans and down-wit-it attitude, an instant shaper-upper of young hoodlums that only works in movies. The students were responding and learning. But that's not, I soon discovered, how it works in LAUSD. A domino effect soon began.

Musical Teachers

Though I was experiencing many problems, I remained pretty happy because I was having success with my students – I mostly could care less about the outside political crap. I just wanted students to learn; at least that was my attitude before the outside came in, and often, to destroy what was going on.

One Wednesday I went to my box to pick up my rosters and the typical daily announcements, and all of the other dailies. Since I had started at Jordan, all of my notes and rosters were addressed to the teacher who held my job previously, though not for my lack of making it known to the proper people. I was told that they would get around to making the name change but, in the meanwhile, I was to "assume all notes to the ex-teacher were for me." It took the school well over a month to put names on my rosters and on my box. And the last time I'd mentioned it to the woman in charge, she blew my hair back, yelling, in front of students and other staff, telling me that I'd never given her my name, though I had, weekly, in writing, in person, upon her request every time. This poor woman was fried from overwork, as most at the school were. It wasn't the last time I was unreasonably chided.

That Wednesday, though, I found a letter apologizing for the fact that the following Monday, less than a week away, I would be moved to another classroom to teach sophomores instead. Other teachers seemed to be in the know, too, and were consoling me, telling me that it would be a good thing, much easier than what I was contending with. I was advised not to cause problems, not even to approach administration, as I had been expressing to my colleagues sadness for my impending move just when I seemed to be making progress. "This stuff happens every week," one teacher had alleged.

I threw a fifteen-minute party for the kids my last day. I made them brownies and unlike my usual classical music – played during journal writing (they bemoaned but quickly became experts on identifying Wagner and Beethoven and were proud of it) – I broke out Blues Travelers (ironically, the song playing was "The Hook Brings You Back"). What a rebel teacher! Five minutes into our party an administrator walked in and told me to turn off the music because someone high up at the district was at the school. I was later told by her not to play music at all. I came to know that "someone higher up at the district is here" was code for "no body is actually here, but passing the buck is easier than taking responsibility for asinine requests."

That Friday I was determined to get to the bottom of the change and find out why music was so, so bad. I went to my Principal, collection of classical music in tow. He thought it was great that I played music but told me, "You aren't leaving your classes. Where'd you get that crazy idea?" He called in the VP and another teacher who was preparing to play musical teachers as well, though she was happy about her change. They threw up their hands and eyeballs when they noticed that my memo was addressed to my predecessor, a man no longer at the school – as though I had received it by mistake and had not taken the time to notice the name. Never mind that the other teacher was given a memo too, addressed properly to her. Never mind either that someone in that room among the four of us, not saying who, concocted this change and signed the friggin' memo! I believe I was blamed for the mess, though I'm not certain. Blaming me was the most decipherable message amidst the red herring mind circus that went on.

I was rushed out before I got the chance to tell them how I'd spent the week preparing for my new classes as well as trying to wrap things up with students who could use a little less change. But I'm glad they rushed me out. I got sleep for the first time that week.

Testing...One, Two

Students are expected to pass periodic district exams. The first one I had to give was during my second week on the job. Our literacy coach came to me the Friday before she wished for me to administer the test, about a week after it was supposed to be given, apologizing for not having come to my classroom earlier. The test was on persuasive writing, a unit that should take about four to six weeks to learn, and I'm talkin' quality weeks: Of the writing types, persuasive is the most difficult, particularly for fourteen-year-olds, and particularly for fourteen-year-olds who have time to study because they have to take care of their babies – yes, and I'm talkin' two-year-old babies who are often kept in the school's daycare. There are many, many obstacles for all the students at Jordan.

The coach told me not to worry, that I wouldn't be held too accountable for the students' failures because she had passed it on to the district that I had just started. At the same time, the coach gave me what seemed a peremptory lecture, treating me as though the impending failures really were a result of my failings as a teacher. At that point, she hadn't witnessed my teaching skills, and never once did she evaluate me while I was at Jordan. She did lots of coaching, however, mainly pointing to her cheeks, telling me to smile at moments when I was pensively looking over literature or trying to follow our Principal's insincere thoughts during staff meetings. But, hey, who am I to complain? Those tax dollars, again, were hard at work. (I hear smiling coaches are big in Japan.)

The test was just another wasted day; students would have benefited from a day of learning. I had just spent a week getting them used to my rules and procedures, of assessing them and getting to know them, of showing them what I expected. Anyone in teaching knows it's important to establish all these things, to set a platform for the learning. When I had planned to dive into the curriculum, planned to drill them and play a marvelous, engaging game to help with basic skills they were lacking, I had to give a test, which would only prove to anyone of reason that if you're not taught it, or don't learn it, you probably don't know it. On paper in some file downtown it could be grounds for my dismissal from the district, eventually. I thought about putting this on tee shirt that week: Testing: Because we have to test, even if it's pointless. Still, this was early on, before I began to be weighted with fighting tremendous battles with higher ups (and everyone's a higher up to a teacher).

The second test I never gave. I was, again, like the first test, given the materials sometime after it was actually supposed to have been given. The same day I was given the test materials, I was given hordes of preparation stuffs for teaching the particular area of language arts to be tested. One of the school's permanent substitutes handed them to me in the hallway, yelling at me in front of my students because she'd been banging on my door for a long time, and I hadn't answered – I'm talkin' in my face screaming. I never answered because we weren't in the classroom, the students and I; we had no chairs. I had taken them elsewhere.

I can't now recall what the test was on. I do remember the stacks and stacks of transparencies that screaming woman handed me, transparencies which should have been provided about six weeks prior, but I was to magically use over one hundred of them and give the test, I kid you not, in one day or two. That's what I was told...oh, and to "do the best I could." I couldn't perform this magic. Surprised? I couldn't use transparencies at all. I'd ordered an overhead, which came to the school (but not to me) weeks after I'd ordered it. I'm now aware that there is a title I warehouse where supplies are kept for low income schools right in Los Angeles with plenty of overheads. I would have picked it up myself, but I needed to go through people who aren't necessarily available.

I kept being told by a very nice man that my overhead was in, but he didn't know where it was and neither did anyone else. Honestly, I don't need an overhead to teach, but the fact that transparencies were given as aids had me busy trying to use them or get what I needed to use them. Those who are trying to help teachers are instead impeding our efforts. I could have wisely spent my time really preparing my students for that test without all this nonsense.

Lockdown Showdown

The second test story coincides with my last few

weeks at the school, when I had to fight my way into the library for lockdown during a racially motivated riot. Many, many events had occurred. I was being given the runaround by the counseling office and those in charge of special education at the school, just to get an Individual Educational Plan request form for a student who had failed all her classes since the sixth grade but had been socially promoted. I began to feel like a tired pawn. I went back and forth between two offices several times to the point where they were laughing at me. I'm glad they thought this student's welfare was so hysterical. I myself enjoy a good laugh, usually not because of one's misfortune, however.

This same student had cussed me out so horribly and so often that the Dean had actually shown up to my classroom to verify the word-for-word referral I had written, something like "This student has repeatedly said the following, as written in every referral given you over the past several weeks: Shut up, you stupid white cunt. You think I'm going to listen to some fucking white stupid cunt? Eat my pussy, you fucking blonde white bitch! I'm not taking out fuckin' paper and fuckin' pen. Fuck you, you fuckin' cunt!" The Dean had assured me that she had been on probation and that this was the last straw for her. She would be given an "Opportunity Transfer," the new, softer way to say she would be kicked out of the school. Why should students actually know they did something wrong? Making them feel shame for wrong action has become the new crime against humanity in the world of teaching. This really conflicts with my own desire that society bring back the Scarlet Letter.

This young lady was in my classroom two days later, so that she could have a new opportunity…to express herself yet again. She did. She was caught writing "fuck you," followed by my name, on my classroom door. I painted over it, and while the paint was still wet, she managed to come back and do it again, an easy thing to do with only one person monitoring the entire building during classes. I was told the student would be arrested for defacing public property. She wasn't.

During this same time, just before the second test episode, students' portfolio binders had finally arrived. They decorated them, and my next step was to guide students toward compiling their work – then, of course, adding to them continuously until summer vacation. Then, on a Monday, I walked in and my chairs had gone missing, all but a few. While my current plan was to work on portfolios, which were left in the classroom and is an activity that requires an actual classroom and preferably a chair or two, we had to go to plan B, again: Find a place for the students to be. For a week, I had to find new places to take my students. Every class was a challenge in finding a place. Most of the time, we were turned away. The Multi-Purpose Room was having an awards ceremony one day. The Librarian wouldn't let me bring my students in without permission first from the administration, but it wouldn't have mattered: "I can't allow more than two classes in here at a time. These teachers got permission days ago." It didn't matter that my students had no place to sit or that there was plenty of room in "his" library.

My room went without chairs for nearly two weeks. (It might still be without chairs). My lesson plans began revolving around the fact that at least half an hour of each hour-long class would be spent finding a place to be. Sometimes we sat on the floor, though students hated that, and I don't blame them. While I swept daily, the wooden, splintered floor was covered in layers of dirt, old gum and U.S.S. (Unidentified Sticky Substances). Sometimes we sat in the stands out in the track field. Sometimes we sat in a grassy area, any grassy area that was dry...or not.

I had been told that tables, which I had requested because I could make better use of the small space in my room, were at the school. Ah! An explanation to the missing chairs! However, the tables were not yet assembled, and nobody knew where they were. I went hunting on my own but never found them. Jordan was becoming for me the Bermuda Triangle for all things needed. When I told students optimistically that we'd soon have tables, they offered to go assemble them. I stupidly offered that up to a superior who laughed at me, and I apologized for offering a solution. Then I tried to explain to my students but didn't have to. They interrupted with "Yeah, we know. We know the way shit works around here. It's just Jordan."

My last Friday, one of my students came to me before the first bell to tell me to stay in my classroom all day. The buzz around campus was that there would be a gang fight immediately following lunch. The previous fall, teachers were injured in a riot, so the young lady was sweetly looking out for me. Near the end of lunch that day, I posted a sign on my door and rerouted my students to the library, which was very nearby. I did not want them stuck in that small classroom with no place to sit for hours during lockdown.

The Librarian stood guard in front of the entrance and did not allow me, or my students, to enter. "You need prior approval from an administrator." I went to get it. As it turns out, my Principal was not on campus that day (Hmmm...). I couldn't find another administrator. None of them were in their offices or visible anywhere on campus, but, and I'm not being sarcastic here, they were working hard and preparing for the inevitable. They were simply, strategically stationed. This time it was I who would get in someone's face.

"There's going to be a riot, now. And my kids are not going to be injured or stuck for hours with no place to sit because of you. Move!"

"But how do you know there's going to be a riot? Kids lie all the time."

"Everybody inside," I'd said, ignoring him.

My students entered the Library just in time. One of my students had run to the window and then shouted back to me, "Lock the doors!"

The smug Librarian told us that he was "the keeper of the keys" and the decision to lock the doors was his. Never mind that when I looked out the window, I saw several cop cars lining the street and the SWAT team members putting on their masks and sprinting across the campus lawn. The Librarian finally took the word of a local policeman who said, "Keep this door locked." It stayed that way for hours, except for the few minutes when the SWAT team stormed the library because a student had thrown a book out the window. I wish I could tell you what was happening on campus, but I never found out.

The following Monday I approached an administrator about the tables or chairs or anyplace that I might take my students to sit. He was defensive and angry that I approached him at all. I went to the main office, requested a sub for the day, and after many days of calling in sick and contemplating the advice to quit, given me by all of my most reasonable friends, I finally did.

Fighting my way into the Library crystallized how every move to help students would be a battle, and I wasn't up for it, as I had thought I might be, at least, not that year, a year that had brought a number of personal losses.

There is so much more to tell about my time at Jordan, so many more battle stories. Every day, moment by moment, there were problems at the school: racism, incompetence, un-professionalism and dishonesty at every level. "If his lips were moving he was lying" was an often-shared fact about our leader, our Principal. I had been subjected also to repetitive, unwanted advances by another teacher. And I am not the only one who has stories like these. I don't think there was more than one teacher on my floor who had planned to return the following year.

While I blame personally anyone who perpetuates racism, I don't blame most of the people at the school for their horrible attitudes. They were overworked; we were understaffed. A mental sickness pervaded the campus. I saw it immediately, and I soon began to feel how it might engulf me, too, if I were to stay on. I think everyone there probably began with good intentions and wound up stuck in gunfight with only a knife, still hoping they could surmount the odds.

Even for me, it's hard to believe that my stories are of only a few months, and they only represent a small fraction of what I experienced. It was difficult to keep in mind with all the nonsense that it's all about the kids. I left mainly because I love teaching, and I didn't want to forget that fact. I knew I would. The interferences and problems were overwhelming.

I'm left with a sense of guilt because while I am free to come and go, those kids from the projects aren't. But the biggest thing I'm left with from my LAUSD experience is this: Teachers are devalued and un-empowered – bottom line. We are trained to keep our mouths shut, and our good intensions – the ones responsible for my guilt – are subverted and exploited. I'm glad to be on the outside. If I were to ever be part of effecting change at LAUSD, this is the only place to be.

Testimonials
of Dorsey Counselors

Los Angeles Unified School District
Susan Miller Dorsey High School

Mr. Roy Romer,
Superintendent of Schools

Ms. Renee Jackson
Superintendent District G

Dr. Evelyn C. Mahmud
Principal

3534 FARMDALE AVE. LOS ANGELES, CALIFORNIA 90016
TELEPHONE: (323) 296-7120 FAX (323) 298-8501

To Whom It May Concern,

This letter is to confirm that Norm Shifren was a teacher at this school and to recommend him in any endeavor he might engage in the future.

Mr. Shifren has a passion seldom seen in educators, and his desire to push students is manifested daily.

Any further questions, please feel free to contact me.

Sincerely,

B. Ching, APSCS

Los Angeles Unified School District
Susan Miller Dorsey High School

Mr. Roy Romer
Superintendent of Schools

Dr. Evelyn C. Mahmud
Principal
3534 FARMDALE AVE. LOS ANGELES, CALIFORNIA 90016
TELEPHONE: (323) 296-7120 FAX (323) 298-8501

December 21, 2002

To Whom It May Concern:

This letter is written at the request of Mr. Shifren, a colleague of mine at Susan Miller Dorsey High School. Mr. Shifren became one of our Spanish teachers this past September. In this short amount of time, I have had the opportunity to see him interact with some of my parents and students.

In conferencing with parents and students, he is very thorough and clear in his classroom/grading expectations. Part of this, is also going over the strengths and weaknesses of the student. In addition, Mr. Shifren makes himself available for questions/tutoring every day.

Mr. Shifren has the genuine want to help students succeed. His aforementioned strengths will be an asset to any educational program or institution.

Sincerely,

Rosario Montoya, Counselor

Susan Miller, Dorsey High School

Los Angeles Unified School District
Susan Miller Dorsey High School

Mr. Roy Romer
Superintendent of Schools

Dr. Evelyn C. Mahmud
Principal
3534 FARMDALE AVE. LOS ANGELES, CALIFORNIA 90016
TELEPHONE: (323) 296-7120 FAX (323) 298-8501

May 28, 2004

To Whom It May Concern:

Norm Shifren and I have collaborated on several occasions
regarding the academic and social progress of students
here at Dorsey High School. He is tactful and always
maintains a high level of professionalism in his interactions. He works hard to maintain strong communication
with students, parents and faculty members,

Mr. Shifren has expressed a sincere desire to work with
students this summer at your institution, and it is my belief
that the students who he interacts with will be well reward-
ed with compassion and a strong knowledge base.

Sincerely,

April M. McNeel
Counselor

Los Angeles Unified School District
Susan Miller Dorsey High School
Mr. Roy Romer

Superintendent of Schools

3534 FARMDALE AVE. LOS ANGELES, CALIFORNIA 90016
TELEPHONE: (323) 296-7120 FAX (323) 298-8501

June 4, 2004

To Whom It May Concern:

I am pleased to recommend Mr. Norm Shifren as a candidate for employment in your program. Mr. Shifren is a foreign language instructor here at Dorsey High School. Mr. Shifren is a teacher who has developed a rapport with his students. Since beginning his permanent teaching assignment he has demonstrated consistent and positive growth. He constantly strives to develop new teaching strategies for the benefit of all his students. He communicates his ideas succinctly, both verbally and in writing. In addition, he works well cooperatively with other staff members and communicates effectively with parents.

Mr. Shifren is a very personable, motivated and hard-working teacher with a clear sense of his instructional goals. He adapts well to new situations and is an innovator in field of foreign language instruction.

It is without any reservation that I recommend Mr. Norm Shifren for employment in your program. I am confident that your organization will be quite satisfied with his job performance.

Sincerely,

Mrs. Daphne McAdoo, School Counselor

Albert Montoya
Susan Miller Dorsey High School
3537 Farmdale Avenue
Los Angeles, CA 90016

(323) 296-7120 ext. 302

June 4, 2004

Letter of Recommendation

Re: Norm Shifren

To Whom It May Concern:

Mr. Shifren has taught Spanish at Dorsey High School for the past two years. In this time, I have had a number of interactions with him. We have been involved in meetings with parents and students. During these meetings, Mr. Shifren has demonstrated how well organized and proficient he is. He is great at documenting and keeping track of all pertinent information. He is always very thorough and is capable of answering all questions that arise during the meetings.

Mr. Shifren shows that he cares a great deal about our students. He sets aside time to tutor students on a regular basis. I have always had positive interactions with Mr. Shifren. I recommend Mr. Shifren to this position. I believe that he will be a good addition to your staff.

Sincerely,

Albert Montoya
School Counselor

October 6, 2002

An open letter from Mr. Shifren, Foreign Language
Department, Dorsey High School to Dr. Evelyn Mahmud,
Principal, Dorsey High School

Subject: Inferences that Mr. Shifren was responsible
for the arson and vandalism burning of 5 classrooms in
building "C" at Dorsey High School

Dear Dr. Mahmud:

During our conference of Thurs., Oct. 3, attended by
UTLA rep Henry Etheridge, you told me that "students
have told you that the arson fire in the C building was
directed at me." You mentioned the my classroom (C-5)
was, in particular, hardest hit with the wiring destroyed,
holes punctured in the walls and ceilings-- all indicating
a personal vendetta toward me. You told Mr. Etheridge
and I that students, totally unsolicited, had offered that the
reason is their dislike of me."

You then showed me a stack of letters from students
and parents, who were unhappy with me, yet when I
asked you for specifics-- i.e., names, context, individual
circumstances, you were not able to produce these.

When we discussed specifics and facts, I told you that
each parent had signed a contract of class rules and
requirements, one of them acknowledging a detailed tardy
policy, and the definition of being on time to class.

During the course of our discussion, I told you that Period
5 was severely affected by a breakdown of classroom
discipline, with zero support from the deans in the most
egregious cases of teacher abuse. I recalled to you a
student who, despite being suspended twice, having had
two parent conferences, a conference with her Magnet
coordinator, and a conference with the assistant principal,
was still abusive, disruptive, and continued to wander
around the room, entering and leaving the class at will, and

inciting others not to follow class instructions.

I recalled to you the fact that on a regular basis, ten to fifteen students would wait until after the tardy bell had rung, and storm into class with food, and drink, and cause absolute anarchy, making it impossible to continue teaching. When I mentioned this to you, your reaction was to make light of my rigid tardy rules. You offered that the proof that the guidelines are dysfunctional is that so many students are tardy. Your suggestion to me in offering a solution was to relax the rules of punctuality, "don't be so hard," your words.

My response to your concept was the following:

"With all due respect, I am a mentor figure for these students. My room is the testing ground for their futures. If there is a lack of proper classroom decorum, where one may run pallmall through the class, displaying disorderly conduct, abusing the teacher, coming into class whenever one desired-- with impunity-- then what is the message I as an educator am imparting? What is my value as a teacher? How can I even begin to teach a foreign language (Spanish), which requires tremendous discipline and consistency, when students can verbally assault me, telling me to "fuck off," are sent to the Dean's office, and then in a "revolving-door" manner, released without any follow-up or actions taken by the deans, only to come back into my classroom to continue their verbal fusillade about who I am to dare send them to the office."

After all this, you're asking me to take the blame for the fire that was set initially to my classroom, because, in your words, "the kids don't like you."

Very truly yours,

Nachum Shifren

Mr. Shifren

Dorsey High School

Foreign Language Department

Mr. Henry Etheridge

UTLA, Dorsey High

December 18, 2002

Re: Harassment and pressure to change grade, lower academic standard, on part of parent and administration

Mr. Etheridge:

On Tues, Dec. 17, 2002, I was called into Mrs. Webb's office to discuss a grade I had given to Reggie Thomas (4th period Spanish). At issue was a request by his mother that I waive a requirement for completing his term paper that was assigned the first week of school and posted on bulletin boards for the last THREE months. Additionally, each parent received and signed the requirement and was therefore aware of all aspects of the project.

The project was due on Dec. 13. The deadline for having me authorize the students' choice of any aspect of Hispanic Culture was Nov. 4. This was done in order to insure that each student would work independently, with no two projects being the same. Also, I am able to monitor and advise the student if the concept was appropriate or feasible, given the parameters of our themes in Hispanic culture and state standards.

The morning of Dec. 13, Reggie turned in his project to me without having my authorization. His claim that he "lost" my authorization is not an issue, since I decided to authorize other projects up to the last week it was due. At no time did he discuss with me his project's feasibility or acceptability or the fact that he had lost my authorization.

Reggie is the only student out of all my classes that did not meet this requirement. He is receiving an " F" grade in Spanish, not having passed one exam in 17 weeks. Additionally, his attitude in class on the whole has been problematic, causing me to move his seat often due to disrupting other students' learning. This has resulted in several office referrals.

My conference with Mrs. Webb and Reggie's mother was a most HUMILIATING experience. I was made to feel like the "bad guy" for not accepting the project, never mind the abovementioned background. Mrs. Webb was insistent that I waive my rules!! When I told Reggie's mother that I wanted to take the report to my room for a moment to check something, she exclaimed excitedly, "I'm afraid of him! I don't trust him!"

I'm being pressured to waive my standards in an outrageous attempt to make me accommodate an unreasonable undercutting of teaching professionalism.

Sincerely, Mr. Shifren

cc. Dr. Mahmud, Roger Scott, UTLA, Dist. G

October 8, 2002

TO WHOM IT MAY CONCERN:

I am writing this letter out of concern for my son, Jonathan Heard, a junior at Dorsey High School. He is currently a student in Mr. Shifren's Spanish 3 class. Upon initial receipt of the syllabus, the outline of the class was good. However, three weeks into the class, the direction of the class changed without any new variations written into the syllabus or any notification given to the student. Along with Spanish 3 classwork, Mr. Shifren started teaching the class Hebrew. He held the students accountable without that being a part of the curriculum. More and more Hebrew was being introduced and less and less Spanish was being covered. Mr. Shifren refused to meet with me concerning this, so I had no other choice but to take my child out of this class. Spanish 3 was not being offered at any other time on campus.

I feel that if a teacher is hired to teach a specific subject, he should be held to this task. As a new parent to Dorsey, I did not know the procedures for holding a teacher to task. I felt at that time the best solution for my child was to remove him from the class because I felt it was not in my child's best interests.

Sincerely,

Stephanie Johnson
Parent of Jonathan Heard

July 23, 2003

Ms. Marguerite P. LaMotte
Board of Education Member
District 1
333 So. Beaudry Avenue, 24th Floor
Los Angeles, CA 90016

Dear Ms. LaMotte:

Congratulations on your victory as the new LAUSD Board member. We're looking forward to meeting and working with you.

Attached to this letter you'll find a letter to Ms. Renee Jackson, a memo to Dr. Evelyn Mahmud, Principal of Dorsey High School, letters, hand written notes by students, and signed petitions regarding a Spanish teacher at Dorsey High School named Mr. Shifrin.   Mr. Shifrin has been a detriment to our students at Dorsey High and LAUSD. He needs to be relieved of his teaching duties at Dorsey and the entire LAUSD school district.

The attachments are self explanatory. The problem has to be solved immediately so our students will not continue to suffer. As parents, we don't want to see him on the Dorsey campus in September.

We've enclosed our cards. Thank you.

Sincerely.

Mrs. Karimu McNeal, Parent Rep.

Mrs. Jacquelyn Smith- Conkleton, Parent Rep.

KM:km

cc: DR. Evelyn Mahmud, Principal
        Ms. Renee Jackson, Local Superintendent
        Mrs. Catherine Webb, Assistant Principal
        Dr. Ching, Assistant Principal
        Mr. Etheredge, U.T.L.A. Chair

        Dorsey High School Parent Group